ON WRITER'S BLOCK

ON
WRITER'S
BLOCK

VICTORIA NELSON

HOUGHTON MIFFLIN COMPANY

Boston   New York   1993

For information about permission to reproduce selections
from this book, write to Permissions, Houghton Mifflin Company,
215 Park Avenue South, New York, New York 10003.

Library of Congress Cataloging-in-Publication Data
Nelson, Victoria, date.
On writer's block : a new approach to creativity / Victoria Nelson.
p.   cm.
Includes index.
ISBN 0-395-64728-2 / ISBN 0-395-64727-4 (PBK.)
1. Writer's block. 2. Creation (Literary, artistic, etc.)
I. Title.
PN171.W74N43 1933   92-38147
808'.001'9 — DC20   CIP

Printed in the United States of America
DOH 10 9 8 7 6 5 4 3 2 1

The author is grateful for permission to quote from the following works: Unpublished poetry by Delmore Schwartz, reprinted by permission, Yale Collection of American Literature, Beinecke Rare Book and Manuscript Library, Yale University. "The Person from Porlock" by Robert Graves, from *Collected Poems* (1961), reprinted by permission of A. P. Watt Ltd on behalf of The Robert Graves Copyright Trust. "Thoughts about the Person from Porlock" by Stevie Smith, from *Collected Poems,* copyright © 1972 by Stevie Smith. Reprinted by permission of New Directions Publishing Corporation. Excerpt from "Youth" by Frances Cornford, from *Collected Poems* (Cresset Press, 1954), reprinted by permission of The Estate of Frances Cornford and Hutchinson Publishing Group Ltd.

For ALN

Contents

———— ❖ ————

June 7. Bad. Wrote nothing today. Tomorrow no time.

— FRANZ KAFKA, *Diaries*

Preface

❖

I N ALL MAJOR FEATURES this book is the same as its first incarnation, published in 1985 by Writer's Digest Books as *Writer's Block and How to Use It*. From the perspective of eight years I have added and modified examples, inserted a new chapter (Chapter 11), refined some precepts, flipped paragraphs around, and polished sentences as all good obsessive revisers must, but on the whole I have changed surprisingly little.

I say "surprisingly" because in the years since its first publication, the principles of humanistic psychology on which this book is based have lost some of their luster in academic circles, while at the same time they have saturated mass audiences via popular therapy and group recovery movements. In particular, the image of the neglected "child" as a major character in our interior landscape has come under attack as a sentimental, ahistorical, anti-intellectual construct. When I put this work under new scrutiny, I wondered if I would recoil from my own blithe and instinctive linking of the child with the "creative unconscious" almost a decade ago.

I did not have this reaction. I feel now the same strong belief in the healing efficacy of the child image that I did the day I first began using it as an aid in conceptualizing the writing process. From my own and others' experiences I conclude that even though the child may have become inconvenient in terms of intellectual respectability, it remains a powerful emblem of all we repress and devalue on a daily basis, both in society and within ourselves. Until that situation changes, the child is going to keep haunting us.

Over the years I have been struck again and again by the perverse reluctance of writers and other artists — thoughtful and educated people, every one — to take into account the most basic principles of human psychology and mental health in the way they approach their work. In the rarefied context of *artiste*-hood, the most garden-variety neurotic behavior is transformed into the exalted aesthetic torment required to forge a tragic vision. Life problems that a building contractor in Idaho with an eighth grade education may be able to deal with directly by joining AA, for example, become badges of honor for "great writers."

Where ignorance of psychology is coupled with artistic self-aggrandizement, writer's block — or, more properly, resistance to writing, a natural element of the creative process — becomes a wonderfully blank screen on which to project the demons whose real territory lies elsewhere in the psyche. It attracts all sorts of notions and self-descriptions that have very little to do with writing itself. The purpose of this book is to dispel some of these illusions and place the act of resistance within the larger context of writing — or, for that matter, of any other act of art, from composing music to glass blowing. For resistance, properly integrated, is one of the great cornerstones of the creative process; it provides a voyage of discovery into the larger issues of writing and self that involve the whole person.

As a manual of applied psychology for artists, then, *On Writer's Block* is written simply, on the grounds that both beginners and those who suffer severe and chronic blocks are experiencing genuine pain. The problem with psychology presented solely as theory is that it distances us from the feeling and ethical dimensions of the writing experience. From pain one wants relief, not more cerebration. The real task in dealing with writer's block is finding the true source of this pain, which often is not a specific problem of writing but the state of the whole organism performing the writing act.

A writer must have the humility to approach his problems as a human being first, an artist second: we cannot enter the graduate school of art before we have graduated from the kindergarten of life. And if we do not grow up, neither will our works. In this sense it is possible to agree with theorists like James Hillman who say that the more truly accepting we are of the child, the less we will be possessed by the notion of recovering it. There is not, finally, much mystery or glamour about the screw-ups of the human condition; there can be only a resolve to approach the unpredictable workings of one's own psyche with honesty and respect.

Who is this writer I have been talking about? In the voices of this book, a writer is I, we, he, she, you, and they — a shape-shifting community of souls with wildly varying temperaments and motives, a community to which my readers and I belong equally. As I noted in the first edition, books that are aimed at helping the "self" characteristically display an I–you polarity ("*I* will help *you*") that is almost always a projection of a dialogue conducted within the author's own mind — in terms of the self being helped, the ultimate Gestalt encounter. It's useful, accordingly, to remember that the "you" is almost always the author herself, the present case being no exception.

On Writer's Block grew directly out of my own experiences as a writer. Years were to pass, however, before *I* grew into *it:* in lifelong ethical tasks the ego always trails behind! As the German playwright Heinrich von Kleist remarked, "It is not *we* who know, it is primarily a certain *state* we are in that knows." Better than any other device, resistance allows us to stumble backward, out of sterile ambition and false goals, into the emptiness that leads directly to that fertile, *knowing* state.

As I wrote in the first version of this book, many colleagues contributed their advice and directed me to specific examples; I have credited their help where possible in the notes. Of special benefit to me were all the volumes in the *Paris Review's Writers at Work* series, surely the most valuable (if not the only) resource on the working habits of twentieth-century writers we have. Alan Andres of Houghton Mifflin supplied enthusiasm and energy in the evolution of the second edition. Finally, I am enormously grateful to all those readers who wrote to me so eloquently after the first edition appeared. May their lives and writings have prospered in the intervening years!

August 6, 1992

ON WRITER'S BLOCK

I

What Writer's Block Means

❖

Without resistance you can do nothing.
— JEAN COCTEAU

T HE PHENOMENON known as writer's block — the
temporary or chronic inability to put words on paper —
is almost universally regarded as a highly undesirable, not to
say unpleasant, experience. It has been called the "unnatural
thwarting of what struggles to come into being, but cannot"
(Tillie Olsen); the "pitiable instance of long incubation producing no chick" (George Eliot). Artists beyond count have
lamented the tortures of this condition, which can strike the
seasoned veteran as unpredictably as it does the beginner.

Writers, when they are not writing, tend to think of themselves in a number of ways, all bad. They are — so they
think — lazy, undisciplined shirkers, failures, cowardly frauds,
good-for-nothings; the list of negatives stretches into cold infinity. Being temporarily unable to write, however — or, for
that matter, to perform any creative endeavor — is not a bad
thing in itself. Properly interpreted, a block is the best thing
that can happen to a writer. Resistance is a vital regulator of
the creative process because it obliges us to suspend our plans
and reconsider the nature of our relation to the creative forces

inside us, forces that are truly gifts — ours by virtue of grace and not possession.

The first of many common misconceptions about writer's block is that it is a neutral state. The truth is that this is no passive condition; it is an aggressive reaction, a loud shout from the unconscious calling attention to the fact that something is out of adjustment. *The block itself is not the problem;* it is a signal to adjust the way we approach our work. By accepting and responding to the message of the block, a writer matures and receives the blessing of the unconscious self, that side of the psyche not directly accessible to us where creative endeavor and a great many other things begin.

The poet Stanley Kunitz said, "The unconscious creates, the ego edits." This is a simple way of looking at the complex relationship between ideas and images that seem to come from nowhere — that is, from the unconscious — and the shaping that the conscious self, or ego (I use these terms interchangeably), gives them once they emerge. Resistance comes from this same unknown territory inside the self; it is a block between the conscious self and its sources of material in the unconscious.

Writers who find themselves unable to produce have made a choice not to write, but they do not experience it as a choice. They perceive their resistance as an externally imposed barrier that has arisen of its own accord. But the fact that the block appears to be involuntary means only that the source of resistance is not conscious; it lies, as it were, on the other side of the barrier. What we call writer's block is a decision of the whole person, made outside the ego's area of control. Although it can be triggered by any number of internal or external stimuli, the vital function that writer's block performs during the creative process remains constant: *inability to write means that the unconscious self is vetoing the program demanded by the conscious ego.* Even as we seem to identify totally with the side of us that says yes, another side is saying no even more forcefully.

Why is it saying no? Why the stubborn lack of cooperation? In desperation our egos manufacture dozens of reasons, mostly self-denigratory, to explain why creativity refuses to flow. But these stereotypical accusations, such as "procrastination," are far from the truth. The key to the dilemma lies not in any failure of will power — blocked writers tend to have more than their fair share of will — but in the relationship we have cultivated with our unconscious selves. This is the unpleasant moment when we learn that this invisible but inalienable inner kingdom runs on its own priorities — priorities that are not always or even often the same as those we hold consciously. If, unwittingly, we break one of those unknown rules, communication between the two realms, inner and outer, is ruthlessly severed and the creative act cannot take place.

Trying to muscle our way past resistance doesn't work either. Picture the unconscious as being a bit like Switzerland, a tough little country with well-defended frontiers and apparently unlimited fiscal reserves. Invasions, coups, don't get past the border. Responding correctly to a writer's block means not forcing an entry but opening civilized diplomatic relations with an autonomous state that has clearly demonstrated it can't be coerced. This is a painstaking process of human negotiation that may take a long, long time.

How is a writer to accomplish the delicate business of getting, and staying, on good terms with the unconscious? Before presenting some suggestions, I offer a short digression on the nature of creativity and its links with a sense of worthiness.

SELF-LOVE AND CREATIVITY

My own heart let me more have pity on; let
Me live to my sad self hereafter kind,
Charitable; not live this tormented mind
With this tormented mind tormenting yet.
— GERARD MANLEY HOPKINS

What is creativity? Above all, it is *play*, the child's fresh spontaneity waiting to come forth in writing or painting or composing music or any other act of art.

Most creative people, and most people generally, remember their childhoods as a time when they threw themselves unselfconsciously and wholeheartedly into all manner of creative efforts: drawing, storytelling, modeling in clay, whatever came to hand. Most important, they experienced no resistance to their play — only the intense, uncritical, unalloyed, and ineffable pleasure of *homo faber*.

One reason that the *idea* of the child has become an emblem for spontaneity, simplicity, and honesty is that it is compensatory to an overload of analytical, ego-oriented thinking. Those who fear that it is a sentimental and anti-intellectual construct are both half right and half wrong. The fact that we still lack the language to describe accurately the workings of the unconscious continues to give power to the idea of the child, as a means not to repudiate rational thinking but to complement and enhance it. And so there remains this quantity inside us to deal with, to integrate, that we find helpful to imagine as a child.

There is, of course, a tremendous difference between the products of art and the products of self-expression. The wellspring of both activities, however, is the same. Writers who want to recapture this joyful spirit from which the hard work of creative endeavor draws its energy must have the humility to recognize, first of all, that they may have forgotten how to play. Luckily, learning how to again is not that hard. One must simply start thinking like a child. If I want to play, do I wait till semester break or summer vacation? Do I wait till I move to the country, away from noisy traffic? Do I wait till my children are grown? Hardly. The child in myself demands emphatically, "I want to have fun *now*. I don't want to wait and I don't see why I should." Viewed from this perspective, procrastination means no more than delaying pleasure, the pleasure to be gained from the playful act of creation.

What's more, no child wants to have fun just during hastily seized spare moments. When I want to play, I want to play for an hour, if not four or five. If I don't have at least one hour, I don't feel alive. And I need it every day. I'm not putting my soul and joy on hold until some vague paradise materializes in my future. If I wait five months or five years to have fun — whether to climb a tree or run down a beach or write — my muscles will be stiff and resistant. I will have throttled my spontaneous desire to play by not giving it free rein on an immediate, regular basis.

An important principle emerges here. Creative discipline grows out of pleasure, not out of tyranny or self-abuse. People who have a strong natural tendency to do what they *like* are those most likely to find discipline an easy responsibility to assume. Their overriding need to satisfy themselves is the solid foundation that sustains them during the long, tedious years of training and effort that a life in art entails.

Loving oneself — as opposed to the narcissism of being *in* love with oneself, with all its attendant insecurities — is one of the most difficult life tasks to master, and it is integrally related to the creative process. One must love oneself to engage in the spontaneous playfulness of the creative act. A person who despises herself will find it difficult to remain squarely on the path of pleasure and to resist the seductive call of lifeless, rigid, self-imposed imperatives.

Having survived the traumas of childhood and the identity crises of adolescence, when self-loathing traditionally reaches its irrational zenith, most of us find something worthy of appreciation in ourselves. Admissions of meager merit, however, are not synonymous with self-love, nor is pride of accomplishment by itself. Writers are achievers, and achievers are people who have been consistently valued — and thus consistently value themselves — for what they do, not for what they are. In the middle of the night, when a lifetime of accomplishments turns into the pitiful antics of a trained pony, the absence of a true sense of worth becomes starkly apparent. Often all we have learned as adults is how to hide, out of sheer self-protection, the extent of our own dis-ease; in the name of modesty and self-sacrifice we go right on abusing ourselves.

Self-love, like writing itself, is not a static condition but an *act* requiring positive moral energy. It is one of the obligations and potential joys of being human. Like writer's block, the absence of love is not a neutral state, either; since Nature abhors a vacuum, love's opposite will move in to fill the empty space. And this self-hatred is a force that must be firmly countered, never surrendered to. Only despair results from giving in to the hateful inner voice that incessantly whispers, "You're no good."

But why, specifically, must one love oneself to write? Because writing, like the other arts, is a fluid, dynamic process; there is nothing rote or mechanical about the act of creation. Carl Jung quotes a precept of medieval alchemy: *Ars requiret totum hominem,* "Art requires the presence of the total being." To keep the total being available means that during the act of composing one must stay in regular touch with the shifting colors and moods of a considerable portion of the psyche. This volatile, continually readjusting contact with self represents the essence of spontaneity — and the opposite of control.

A writer who taps a large hidden reservoir of self-hatred every time he makes deep contact with himself is not likely to want to tarry in the mode of self-communion. Instead, he will find himself mysteriously "blocked." What has actually happened is a little more complicated: in a split second the writer has thrown up the block — that is, retreated from the deep self-communion necessary to perform a creative act — to shield himself from a withering blast of hatred from within. The despised block is actually a positive form of self-protection — primitive, certainly, but a reaction to an even more primitive emotion. And no other form of protection is available to a person who consciously denies the existence of, or refuses to come to terms with, deeply ingrained habits of self-laceration.

Like all unconscious defenses, however, this kind of global paralysis leads only in a circle and refuels the very fires of self-loathing it tries to save a person from. Thus, although writer's block is a deeply healthy and self-protective act, true progress cannot begin until the hatred is acknowledged on a more conscious level of the psyche. To be free to play, the writer must have the conscious strength, not simply the unconscious reflex, to keep the demons at bay.

Learning to protect oneself directly instead of indirectly through a creative block means, in the simplest terms, that one must learn to love oneself. For the *totum hominem*, this is the moral task of a lifetime. In writerly terms it can be addressed just as simply. To function as a writer, one must, above all, love and honor one's creative force, which can be pictured — in what has become a pervasive metaphor of our era — as a kind of childlike spirit.

Whether it is a brand-new presence or a lifelong companion, we must be very gentle and respectful with this entity. We must not keep it chained up in a dark closet or force it to perform a never-ending routine of distasteful chores. We must let it out to play, as all children desire to do; we must let it follow, with loving and nonintrusive guidance, its own inclinations.

A writer who is harsh and unreasonably demanding of this child will eventually be stuck with a sullen, rebellious, never-to-mature adolescent who refuses to clean up his room or do the dishes; thus has her creative soul been bred and reared. But if the writer has been a wise and gentle parent, the child will prosper and reward him in ways the narrow adult ego could never believe possible.

Framed in these terms, when a writer experiences a block it means that the child is throwing herself on the floor and refusing to cooperate. What should the parent do? Try to compel the child, kicking and screaming, to do what she would not? Send her to her room without dinner? Give her a number of logical reasons why she *ought* to cooperate? Or try to find out why she doesn't want to in the first place? The key lies in what the child has been asked to do and how the request has been made. Has the child been asked only to play? Not likely. More often he has been commanded to perform brain surgery or recite Shakespeare. Has he been enrolled in graduate school, which, at the age of three, he does not feel quite ready to attend? In other words, have unrealistic expectations been imposed on a creature whose true potential may lie in a direction completely overlooked by his writer-parent? Who is the real child here?

This classic conflict between the ego and the unconscious demonstrates an interesting fact: we tend to be much kinder to other people — our friends, relatives, and offspring — than we are to ourselves, to whom, in the dingy privacy of our inner lives, we often behave like little dictators. In most cases, writer's block is the child's healthy scream of pain or rebellion against outrageous totalitarian treatment or blasting self-hatred, two sides of the same sad coin. Artists who remain internally polarized in this way cannot perform the fine discrimination and weighing of unconscious messages that are vital to the creative effort. The nuanced courtship of self, the subtle give and take, the advances and retreats that make up a typical creative experience dissolve instead into that dull gray monolith the Block.

Discipline has to be acquired eventually — the child *must* go to the dentist, after all — but it should not be perverted into another occasion for self-loathing. True creative discipline — and productivity — blossoms in conditions of gentleness and respect. Note, however, that the conditions of creativity are not synonymous with its results: self-love is not the same as adopting a tone of optimism in one's work. Gloomy, despairing works of art as well as "cheerful" ones are the product of a positive relationship between conscious and unconscious in the artist's psyche. And those writers whose self-esteem does not seem manifestly high, who have still managed, despite great suffering and self-torture, to produce a body of significant work, can be said to have triumphed over their own disabilities. They have experienced self-integration in the creative act itself.

To maintain the delicate equilibrium between ego and unconscious, each writer needs to give careful attention to the unique "personality" of his creative nature. Sometimes a writer must tear up the application to graduate school (that is, an overambitious project) as being beyond his child's present capabilities. Other times, he must realize that, out of a critical lack of self-confidence he has forced his postdoctoral-level creative energies to endure the ignominy of kindergarten! It is also essential to employ the conscious ego to distinguish between the infantile, destructive, child*ish* and the inspired, playful, child*like* workings of the unconscious. Only by a meticulous "sorting of the seeds," as the Jungians say — into wheat and chaff — can we determine the appropriate creative response to each situation. Such careful discrimination is not possible if we do not love ourselves. Paradoxically, only affection yields the balance and detachment needed to understand and judge the messages we receive from the unconscious.

Engaging in an act of art is very much like establishing a relationship with another person. If you try to possess or control that person, he or she will elude you; if, instead, you form a friendship based on mutual respect, then over time, with much love and patience, you can forge a secure bond. To accomplish this goal, however, you must be prepared to effect a fundamental change of attitude toward yourself. At the root of all practical prescriptions must be a turning around, an opening up of new possibilities in the self, an infusion of that positive spirit without which all life activities seem, as they did to a certain well-known character, "stale, flat, and unprofitable."

Such a metamorphosis will not take place as a result of a New Year's resolution. Love, of oneself as much as of another, still remains an act of grace, not a conscious, willed decision. It is something not to be compelled but to be relaxed into. When the miracle happens (and it is an easy miracle, if only you allow it), the writer finds a different reality before him. With eyes newly opened he sees that what seemed a barrier — resistance — is actually the secret door to the unconscious. If he hurls himself against it, he will only succeed in bruising himself. If he approaches with love and careful attention, it will open of its own accord. This is the way in which writers discover that the block is actually a building block in their unfolding development — that resistance is an essential component, not the final chapter, in their creative lives.

2

Starting Cold:
The Beginner's Block

———— ❖ ————

Times of growth are beset with difficulties. They resemble a
first birth. But these difficulties arise from the very profusion of
all that is struggling to attain form. Everything is in motion;
therefore, if one perseveres there is a prospect of great success,
in spite of the existing danger.

— RICHARD WILHELM,
Commentary on the *I Ching*, Hexagram 3,
"Difficulty at the Beginning"

L ET US BEGIN at the beginning — of a writing project,
of a life in writing. The problem facing most writers who
are setting out — the experienced writer who must begin at
zero with each new work as much as the learner and apprentice
— is simply this: Why is it so hard to start writing? And why,
especially, is it so hard to *start* to start?

As I sit at my desk facing an empty page, a thousand
thoughts race through my head. Out of that whirling grab bag
of possibilities, how do I *choose*, pick one word or the other,
violate the virgin blankness of the paper with a pitifully inadequate rendering of my complex imaginings? No, thank you, I
decide. Easier to keep the thoughts in my mind, spare the

snowy white paper, avoid the discouraging compromise between intent and technical ability that is the written word.

So goes a certain mood familiar to all who would and do
write. This gentle daydream, however, is the true violation of
a writer's spirit and talent. The bravest act a writer can perform is to take that tiny step forward, put down the wretched
little word that pricks the balloon of inflated fantasies with its
very mundanity, and then put down another word directly after
it. This act marks the decision to be a writer. That first word
put on paper bridges the gulf between the person who imagines what it is like to write and the person who writes.

Not everyone with a desire to write, after all, becomes a
writer, and that is not necessarily because of a lack of inherent
talent or an inability to communicate with words. Many avid
readers harbor a secret desire to be a writer because they
believe that the pleasure to be gained from writing is identical
to that gained from reading. But to be a writer, a person must
first actually write, and write a great deal.

If this definition sounds simpleminded, consider. A long-
distance runner is someone who runs. Runs long distances, in
fact. A long-distance runner is not a person who *desires* to run.
A long-distance runner actually runs, and usually every day. If
I announce to my friends that I want to run the Boston marathon, they might reasonably ask, "What steps are you taking to
achieve this goal?" I might answer, "Well, I'm training ten
miles every other day this year. I want to run a few fourteen-
kilometer races first to see how I do under pressure. Next year
I'll increase my training to fifteen miles. If I can maintain that
distance at a good time for another year, maybe then I'll be
ready."

But suppose I answer instead, "I'm not running at all right
now. I just thought I'd like to try it." Pressed further, I admit,
"I thought I'd start with the Boston marathon to see if I like
running or not." My friends might justifiably consider me not
merely mad but a likely candidate for shin splints or a heart
attack. Just think, then, how benevolently we let slide in casual

conversation that famous wish-announcement: "I've got a novel in me. Someday I'm going to write it."

I do not attack the earnest desire to communicate to others a life story full of hard-won truths. But I do argue with the image. A novel is something that stands at the end of a lengthy process called writing. It is not a preexisting Platonic form embedded within the writer, only waiting (as some would put it) to be "dialogued." I do not have a Boston marathon inside me waiting to get out. The marathon is a peak experience I am rightly entitled to look forward to only as the culmination of years of regular training and love of running.

But running, it might be argued, is essentially a matter of performance; it is not a creative act. If writing were only the mechanical business of putting one foot in front of the other, there would be no writer's block. This is true. The *act* of writing, however, is performance. During this act a writer is not so much "translating" an idea into words as she is creating the idea in the shape of the words that present themselves to her. As the poet William Stafford said, "A writer is not so much someone who has something to say as he is someone who has found a process that will bring about new things he would not have thought of if he had not started to say them." The words, in effect, create the idea. The result — play, story, poem — records the act of creation. It is emphatically not a prize the writer captures once he gets through the tedium of "dialoguing." The chores *are* the prize. They're all you get.

A novel, as we think of it in our culture, is composed of perhaps ten thousand carefully crafted sentences. The shaping of each of those sentences is what the craft of writing is about. Philip Roth has his distinguished author declare in *The Ghost Writer:*

> I turn sentences around. That's my life. I write a sentence and then I turn it around. Then I look at it and I turn it around again. Then I have lunch. Then I come back in and write another sentence. Then I have tea and turn the new sentence around. Then I read the two sentences over and turn them

both around. Then I lie down on my sofa and think. Then I get up and throw them out and start from the beginning. And if I knock off from this routine for as long as a day, I'm frantic with boredom and a sense of waste.

This is the nuts and bolts of the writing experience. And a person must love (or perhaps more accurately, be compelled into) repeating this narrow and exacting task ten thousand times before he will have produced a novel.

Once again the word "love." This type of love, though, is directed toward an activity as well as toward oneself. How can I run a marathon if I don't intrinsically love the act of running for its own sake? Only the fact that I love to run — around the track, whenever I can seize the opportunity — will carry me through the years of grinding practice necessary to develop my running powers to their full capacity. The core of the running or the writing experience is pleasure in the act. It sweetens the tedium of training; it carries me on, lighthearted, to my goal.

Still, there's no getting around it. That first encounter with the blank page is a terrible, anxiety-ridden moment, a nerve-racking trial at any point in a writer's life. It is possibly hardest, however, for the person either new to writing or returning after an extended absence. For the beginner, the paralysis that comes from starting cold is usually a "developmental" phenomenon, as the child psychologists say; with time and practice, it often subsides to a tolerable (though still trying) level of anxiety. Chronic, or recurring, blocks and situational blocks that grow out of a specific writing context will be taken up in later chapters.

For many, this first experience of writer's block is definitive. They get right up from the desk and never come back, and they are correct and honest to do so. They have sent themselves a message so unmistakable that they would be foolish and wrongheaded to persevere or to experience a moment's guilt for their decision. For this large and honorable portion of the population, the writer's block, properly interpreted, opens a door to a bright future, albeit a different one than they had anticipated. It has told them that despite the demands of their ego, there is *something else* out there they would rather be doing than writing. And they are now free to go find this thing, and do it.

Others are slower on the uptake. Camped at the doorstep of writing, blocking themselves aggressively and intentionally from entry but unable to make the decision to turn away, they become Ancient Mariners of the writing world. Persons permanently stalemated here, before they have written enough to qualify as *writers* with writer's block, tend to display this symptom as the most visible sign of a more generalized compulsive neurosis in which the desire to perform a given act is pitted against the refusal to do so in many areas of life. Such an impasse is often linked to a fear of maturity and accomplishment. The ultimate goal of this elaborately designed ritual is to increase the self-loathing of the sufferer and to divert his or her attention from the true source of misery, which is generally something entirely removed from the writing sphere.

There is the case of a man who, coming late to college, was driven by compulsive fears that he had failed in life and always would. Accordingly, he focused an inappropriately massive attention on every scrap of learning material that came under his gaze. He quickly fell under the spell of two books he was assigned in literature classes, *Lord of the Flies* and *Steppenwolf.* Immersing himself in these works, he devised an elaborate metaphysical theory that explained both the novels and his own relation to the universe. At term's end he found himself unable to convey this complex tangle of interlocking ideas in the required two five-page book reports. He was unable, in fact, to set down a single sentence from his huge and well-thumbed stack of index cards. Taking incompletes in both courses, he tortured himself nightly for the next two years, poring fruitlessly over his notes, hopelessly blocked. The papers were never written. He had loaded them with the burden of doing what he could not do himself, and his unconscious quite rightly refused to have the responsibility for redemption shunted onto its shoulders.

What this man had cleverly hit upon was a way to carry over his deep self-loathing into the academic environment, where he had begun to show signs of promise. His true source of misery was not the inability to write a paper but a more extensive personality confusion that chose the medium of a writer's block as a way of wounding him again with failure, of dragging him back to the past just as his future showed a modest brightening. And as long as he saw himself as the passive victim of a "block," he did not need to confront his own active role in causing himself grief.

This syndrome is neither so extreme nor so unusual as we might wish it to be. Almost every writer, at the outset of his or her creative adventure, has at least briefly fallen victim to this type of obsessive behavior. It is a chilling illustration of the paralysis that may result at any stage of a writing life when the first causes that trigger a block are not directly identified and examined. To experience a block unconsciously is to *be* the block; to value it as a legitimate response and seek to bring its true source into consciousness is to open the door to a range of paths on which to move forward.

VOICES FROM THE PAST

One of the commonest mundane disguises of self-hatred that engender a protective block is the sensation a writer has, not of cooperating with a childlike part of himself, but rather of *being* a child beset by horribly critical authority figures whenever he ventures to perform the act of art.

True writer's block is not a phenomenon of childhood. As a rule, young children don't complain of wanting to fingerpaint but finding themselves mysteriously unable to do so. Children either write spontaneously because they like to or don't write because they don't like to. In school, the desire to write a story or poem may take a bad turn, and an overcritical or narrow-minded teacher may freeze a child's natural instincts toward self-expression. Many highly literate people can trace their disinclination to write to a critical teacher or overly demanding parent.

Such people, when they are not writers by profession, have neither the incentive nor the need to learn how to integrate a resistance that rests at the periphery of their lives. They may have difficulty writing memos or letters, but the block in these cases is merely a minor annoyance. On the other hand, *writers* who have internalized from their pasts a witch or tyrant who despises their every word have the moral obligation to face up to this childhood ghost. For although it is right and justified that a child should feel terrified of such a real person in his life, a grown-up does not need to feel the same way thirty years later. And it is fatal to do so.

When I am sitting in my room "trying" to write, as we like to say, who is actually physically present? Not the tormenting Mr. X or Mrs. Y, certainly, even if they are still alive. The only person in that room is me. And the only honest conclusion I can draw from this fact is that a part of me is now Mrs. Y or Mr. X, and that part of me hates me and is my mortal enemy. Yet even as "I" submit passively to a torrent of abuse about my efforts, still another part of me, that healthier child, is having no part of it, and he shuts down the shop until the climate turns a little more inviting. "I," mistaking this defense for recalcitrance, laziness, and the like (Mrs. Y is ready with a few labels), then join forces with my enemy to wage fruitless battle against my friend.

To become a conscious person, and to become a writer fully responsive to the inner dynamics of creation, I must recognize that the world inside me contains a whole cast of characters, not all of whom are nice people but all of whom belong to me. I must realize, as the Welsh fantasist Arthur Machen once put it, that "the human soul, so far from being one and indivisible, might possibly turn out to be a mere polity, a state in which dwelt many strange and incongruous citizens, whose characters were not merely unknown but altogether unsurmised by that form of consciousness which so rashly assumed that it was not only the president of the republic but also its sole citizen."

If these inner players are not to rule my life, I must — just as I do in my outer life — determine who is on my side and form my allegiances accordingly. Identifying my self-hatred is the first step in taking responsibility for having generated this hatred and criticism. I cannot stand up to something I have not identified. As long as it is attached to some cardboard figure from the past and I passively accept its judgments as a vehicle of truth, my demon has succeeded in fooling me and I will never be able to confront him directly.

"It is not given to us to choose whether we are happy or unhappy," the writer Natalia Ginzburg said. "But we must choose not to be *demonically* unhappy."

GETTING SERIOUS

A less sinister mental attitude that is likely to trip up the unwary novice writer intent on plunging ahead is the fallacy of "getting serious." Apprentice writers who have reached the stage where they wish to focus their energies intently and concentrate on developing their abilities often paradoxically experience this moment as expulsion from Eden. The apple has been bitten; self-consciousness enters the picture. They decide, to their eternal loss, that henceforth they are no longer to Play, they are to Write.

This decision has a distinctly silencing effect on that other part of you who still wants nothing more than to keep on playing. He does not want to be sent to military school, and he refuses to cooperate in this mad plan. That is the message he sends back to you, in the form of a writer's block, when you suddenly interrupt his play by rapping out a command to Write.

What is the best response to this situation? The answer is unequivocal: don't give the child (and yourself) a severe thrashing. That won't enhance his desire to attend military school. Instead, apologize sincerely, throw away the little uniform, and give him back his toys. Do not try to make your fragile budding talent carry prematurely the extra weight of seriousness. This thinking applies equally to experienced writers, who can strangle themselves just as effectively with an exaggerated sense of their importance to literature.

Translated into the reality of the writing life, what does giving back the toys mean? It means that, for example, you will not try to switch your subject matter to an area that seems more suitable for a great writer. You will not forswear your accustomed mode of expression because you don't think it sounds important enough. Your new sense of commitment must not be allowed to change the nature of what you are doing, nor hasten its growth artificially. Your writing will develop more naturally if you resist the temptation, for the time being, to crown yourself Writer and continue simply to think of yourself as someone who is playing around. Remember that the despised word "dilettante" comes from the Italian *dilettare*, to delight in.

THE QUESTION OF TIME

An important early step in becoming a writer is learning how to allocate *time* in your life for writing. Misuse of time is more likely to inhibit writing than any other single factor.

Even to utter the word "misuse," I know, is likely to trigger an avalanche of guilty, self-blaming thoughts in you, my writerly reader. Let me make my meaning clear. Most writers believe that misuse of time means not spending enough time working. I believe the reverse. We abuse time far more often by attempting to be unrealistically strict with ourselves than by being too lazy. Laziness or procrastination in writing is almost always the direct response to an internal edict that is far too severe. It is the same yo-yo behavior apparent in the dieting-overeating phenomenon. Instead of embarking on a positive program of healthy eating, dedicated dieters put themselves on a gulag routine of fasting, with occasional breaks for carrots and broth. This extreme maltreatment of the organism results, in time, in its antithesis: an orgy of chocolate-cake eating. Similarly, the attempt to impose on oneself a stringent regime of writing usually produces its direct opposite, no writing at all. The psyche revolts against harsh new habits.

Beginners are often the most unrealistic in their use of time, if only because their expectations of what they will be able to produce are as yet untested. They have still to learn their natural capacity and rhythm in writing. If they have Gotten Serious to boot, they are likely to abandon the unselfconscious writing patterns of the past and embark on an overambitious program that can freeze them up harder than Lake Baikal.

This block may also strike those who write in exhausting spurts — who, given the choice of any time at all to write, will closet themselves dramatically from Friday morning to Tuesday afternoon instead of going out and having fun on the weekend like any right-minded individual. Less frivolously, someone who is starting her writing life while holding a full-time job is obliged to set loose her child to play during times she might prefer to spend relaxing. Many writers, even those not obliged to do so, find the middle of the night an exciting creative period; the time selected for writing is a very personal choice. But often the body and emotions rebel against any forced labor by refusing to let their master write again for an unpredictably long period of time, after which the whole exhausting cycle will start up again. In terms of plain animal comfort and long-term endurance, there is much to be said for a regular daily routine.

Many beginning writers do work sporadically at first. This is a natural way to ease oneself into a creative medium. Gradually the writing act gathers momentum and over time settles into a semiregular routine. Often, however, it takes five to seven years of writing before a writer is equal to (and more important, looks forward to) a daily routine. During those years, thanks to gentle care, the playful child has had the time and space to mature into a responsible young person ready to start college while holding a part-time job — a staunch ally in place of the lazy, rebellious indentured servant that self-contempt creates.

To part company with the old adage, inspiration rather than perspiration may have to be your guide at the beginning. Journalists, technical writers, and a category of serious prose writers who might be labeled "macho professionals" jeer at such a notion, but theirs is quite a different skill (and often sets off a massive block of its own when the old pro secretly tires of cranking out formulaic prose). The person who is beginning to produce imaginative writing will almost always find the track extremely faint and hard to follow at first.

If you are experiencing a high level of resistance at this early stage, you must make an extra effort to keep as close as possible to your original pursuit of pleasure and the spirit of play. You must focus strongly on locating your desire: you must write when you *want* to write. As your writing muscles develop at their own not-to-be-hurried rate — perhaps quickly, but more likely very slowly — you will find yourself able to write with greater technical facility. This increase in your powers produces a tremendous feeling of pleasure and accomplishment, which in turn motivates you in the best way (and far more solidly than outside praise) to persevere in your efforts.

The single most common mistake in setting up a writing schedule — one that, unbelievably, even experienced writers con themselves into committing — is to announce proudly, "Well, my schedule is too full at the moment to do any writing, unfortunately. But come semester break/summer vacation/retirement/Christmas, I will have eight hours a day to write, write, write!" Surely no faster way to trigger inner resistance has yet been devised by humankind. Comes the long-awaited time, the eager neophyte sits down at her desk and — nothing. A total blank. Why? Because, after cutting out all training (and fun) for a lengthy period of time, she is sitting down to the emotional and creative equivalent of the Boston marathon. Inside her, the child is writhing in anguish that she has so mistreated him by setting such a difficult task. Run the marathon cold? No, thanks.

Thinking about writing is an activity that produces its own brand of pleasure. Writing itself, like ballet dancing, is a completely different task that requires regular practice for ease of performance. The less you do, the harder it gets. In anticipation of a long free stretch of time, if only to remember what it actually feels like, you should be writing regularly. If you fail to perform this simple act of preparation, you will waste a great deal of that free time engaged in the most basic retraining activities.

To keep writing an integral part of "regular" life, as opposed to a blocked and unsatisfactory holiday activity, is absolutely vital. But how can a busy daily schedule involving the earning of wages and the rearing of children be unraveled to allow time for writing? Here it's necessary to say the obvious: we always find time to do the things we genuinely like doing. As Fritz Perls said, "The organism does not *make decisions.* The organism works always on the basis of *preference.*" We can, however, use logic as a way to identify true, as opposed to illusory, preferences. The following questions, honestly answered, are directed to that end.

1. Can unnecessary items be cut out of my busy schedule to give me time to write? (If your answer is yes, you have your time and you can try it out tomorrow. If your answer is no, proceed.)

2. Is my schedule going to be this full for the next year? (If your answer is no, then wait until the time opens up, but take writing opportunities along the way as frequently as possible. A year is really the outer limit. If your answer is yes, proceed.)

3. Have I made an unconscious choice — that is, have I decided *against* writing as part of my daily experience, just by having this kind of life? (If your answer is yes, proceed.)

4. What unrealized hopes or fantasies does my desire to write actually stand for, and how can they be realized in my life *as I am living it this very moment?*

It's important to realize that "wanting to write" is a time-honored fantasy for many, equivalent to escaping to a desert island. This is harmless daydreaming that turns ugly only when the dreamer begins judging his fantasy by real-world standards that patently don't apply: "I keep thinking about writing but never do it, therefore I'm a failure and a fraud." Then it is time to ask what void in real life this fantasy attempts to fill. Often it is simply freedom from daily responsibilities and a sterile work environment. These constraints can be eased in ways entirely unrelated to writing, which carries its own staggering set of daily responsibilities, financial worries, and drudgery.

But consider question 3 again. What if you answered no? What if you are determined to write in spite of an overwhelmingly busy life? Some — very few — take responsibility for their time allocations in the following way: "I must keep this schedule because other lives depend on my earning a livelihood, but in spite of all odds I will carve out an hour or two every day for myself because I *want* to write." This decision requires sacrifice, stamina, and a special kind of courage to keep both the adult and the child well and happy. It represents a crucial turning point at which a small number of developing writers emerge from the ranks of those who merely desire to write.

A ROOM OF ONE'S OWN

Virginia Woolf listed as a primary requirement of the writer an inviolable space in which to be alone with one's thoughts and words. Such a clearly defined work territory is unquestionably essential to the development of most writers. Very few — Jane Austen is one of the famous exceptions — have been able to go about their business successfully with other people in the same room performing their daily tasks. But there is no need to be too narrowly literal or literary in interpreting what this space should be in your life.

For the person starting out, a desk consecrated to writing

can be a soothing talismanic object that offers protection against the fear that rises during beginnings. In these critical moments even the prospect of having to take paper and notes out of storage can seem sufficient reason to postpone the endeavor indefinitely. Sometimes it's easier to start playing if the toys are already laid out.

Some writers, feeling a need for greater privacy, rent a room or garage in someone else's house, go to a writers' colony, or find the proverbial cabin in the woods. While these alternatives are a necessity for some, they do not work for all. Even for an experienced writer, it can be as risky to divorce the place of writing from regular life as it is to divorce the time. This restriction of the writing experience to a region vacuum-sealed from daily affairs tends to give it that dreaded "special" aura that can lead to a first-class writer's block. The formidable weight of literary tradition descends the instant you walk into the pristine sanctum lacking telephone, dirty socks, newspapers, all the comforting links to the outside world. Most writers need the strong, enduring emotional and social ties of everyday life to balance the long hours spent working in solitude. Walden Pond, after all, was within easy walking distance of Concord. Writing is a lonely vocation. By putting themselves in a lonely environment as well, some writers risk turning Prospero's cell into a padded one.

Often the illusion persists that if one weren't surrounded by family, duty, business, and other distractions, a great flood of creativity would be released. Getting away from the routines and setting of the ordinary can have a wonderfully vivifying effect on a writer's work — and spirits. The writer's retreat sometimes offers the *only* possibility for uninterrupted concentration needed to begin a new project. Some writers, however, when they finally get to the colony, may be crushed to discover that their new surroundings make no difference at all — that they continue to put in the same hour or so a day (or even, more humiliatingly, every *other* day) that they did with all the chaos of daily life around them. If you are this kind of writer, you have made an important discovery: You are not *blocked* simply because you write only so much per day. This is your internal rhythm that functions regardless of your environment. Learn to value and accept it.

If you are still determined to try your cabin in the woods, consider two preemptive strategies: (1) to avoid stage fright and the rigors of a cold, untrained-for-the-marathon start-up, make sure you have your new project well under way before you begin packing your bags; (2) consider taking a spouse or friend with you, for it is often a mistake to go alone. As any peasant can tell you, the wilderness is full of demons that feed on the souls of solitary humans. If you are planning only to chop wood and set up a primitive living situation, you are not likely to be bothered by them, being too occupied with material concerns. But if you are going with the sole intent of tuning in to your unconscious, you may be swallowed up by what comes out. Worse, you may be bored and frustrated most of the time — what else is there to do, after all? Writing is not a twenty-four-hour occupation.

Many writers do flourish in this setting, composing whole drafts of books in six weeks' time or performing other prodigious creative feats. It's important to realize, though, that the cabin-in-the-woods stereotype is just that — a collective shoe that may not fit your foot. If it pinches, why force yourself to wear it? Often such attempts at isolating yourself are merely another disguise for your ego's efforts to *compel*, rather than allow, writing. You think: Up there with nothing else to do, I'll have to write, right? Wrong. Far from being alone with your work, you are much more likely to be alone with your compulsion *not* to write.

WARMING UP

Most writers starting out find that it's the shock of using new muscles, of having no idea what they're capable of, that freezes their nerve at the outset. The less you have done of something, after all, the harder it is to do. This initial painful hesitation is a function of development; writers outgrow it as they become more facile with the written word. The beginner's block and the stage fright that produces it are gradually eased (though do not expect them ever to go away completely!) with practice and experience. For this easing to take place, however, the would-be writer must gather the courage to step over the threshold and begin to write. There is no other way.

How is this to happen? For those beginning and other writers who have hurled themselves again and again at the door only to have it slammed in their faces, the problem of starting cold has an easy remedy: warming up. When the writing muscles are out of shape and a certain amount of self-wounding from fruitless attempts to begin has already occurred, it is wise to proceed slowly.

Warming up means learning to play like a child again and consists of the following easy steps. First, allow yourself to do nothing at all until you feel a deep and genuine urge to write something specific. Then write only *what* you want to. Write *where* and *when* you want to. Write as much or as little as you like. When you get tired of writing, quit.

Deliberately reapproaching your writing in this way can be helpful whenever you experience resistance to writing according to a preconceived regimen. Warm up with any kind of writing that comes easily. Make believe you are a child again, doing only what you love to do, what gives you pleasure. Go always in the direction in which you instinctively feel the strongest pull, regardless of whether your ego judges this to be the "right" sort of writing. Your instincts and your talent want to flow in this direction, so let them — let the river find its natural course. Whatever you create, make sure the experience gives you the most satisfaction and fun. What's important to remember is that you're just fooling around. What you're doing isn't serious. It "doesn't count." It's play.

Many joys can be derived from these early stages of writing. For one, beginners who are not yet broken into the yoke of a writing "career" can enjoy all the spiritual rewards of writing with none of its considerable real-world drawbacks. Beginning writers have not yet begun to worry about repeating themselves. They can experiment, fall down, be silly, and do unexpectedly wonderful things outside the glare of public criticism. They are truly writing for themselves and no one else.

During these early years, as you are discovering how, what and under which conditions you prefer to write, keep your attention firmly fixed on the excitement and difficulties of each moment of writing, on the specific problem you are grappling with or the passage you are able to raise to its full level of expression — and what a triumph that is. You are limbering up and toning your creative muscles. Relax and enjoy it. Do not try to look too far ahead or you will be paralyzed by the prospect of possible achievements you are not nearly ready to make. Respect your own efforts, feeble as they will undoubtedly seem from time to time. Most writers start from zero, and it is far easier to get better than it is to get worse.

Above all, remember that attitude is far more important than time or place. Do your writing where and when you *prefer*, for preference is the foundation of routine and not the other way around. Remember your silent partner in the undertaking, whose function is to keep you honest as well as inspired. If you approach writing as a hallowed mission or a vehicle for your need to be important, your desire to write will shrivel inside you. Approach writing in a relaxed and spontaneous manner, and your desire will not desert you.

In the beginning, before it was duty, art was child's play.

3
The Myth of Procrastination

———— ❖ ————

In the meantime I had got myself entangled in the old sorites
of the old sophist — procrastination. I had suffered my necessary business to accumulate so terribly that I neglected to write
to any one, till the pain I suffered from not writing made me
waste as many hours in dreaming about it as would have suf-
ficed for the letter-writing of half a life.
— SAMUEL TAYLOR COLERIDGE

L ET US TAKE the case of a writer who is past the "starting block," a writer who has begun to work seriously and
has accumulated a small but growing body of work. Yet this
writer keeps being troubled by a nagging resistance to getting
down to it. Worse still — and it is by no means an uncommon
experience — this writer has spent the last twenty-five or thirty
years trying, in effect, to "push the river," because her personal river of creativity, contrary to all natural laws, shows no
signs of wanting to flow by itself. What work she has actually
managed to finish either stands as a sweaty monument to will
power or was produced, seemingly by accident, in various unscheduled moments of grace that no amount of wishing or
forcing seems able to conjure up again.

Over the long haul, if resistance to writing develops into a
chronic state, it becomes far more difficult to resolve than

beginner's block. By this point writer's block has hardened into an ingrained response, as habitual as smoking or overeating, and it must be approached at a correspondingly deep level in the psyche — a level that such devices as the New Year's resolution never penetrate. In fact, the New Year's resolution, also known as will power, plays an integral part in perpetuating the whole frustrating cycle. Writer's block is far more frequently found in the presence of too much, not too little, will.

There is a terrible perversity, which the blocked writer is all too aware of, in not doing what one seems to desire most to do. Yet once again, *not* wanting to write is, under certain crucial circumstances, as healthy and natural an impulse as the act of writing itself. Notice that I have said "not wanting" to write. Usually the sufferer phrases it differently: "I want to write, but I *can't.*" For our purposes, it is more productive to accept the block for precisely what it is and say, "At the moment I don't *want* to write." Only by taking direct responsibility for this state of affairs can you proceed to (1) discover why you don't want to write — no, why you *refuse* to write (there is almost always an excellent reason that is a credit to your unconscious integrity) — and then (2) determine whether an alternative path to writing is available. Although some of the reasons you uncover may derive simply from specific technical problems you are experiencing with a manuscript, the deepest, most pervasive cause of chronic writer's block has nothing whatever to do with writing itself.

What is this cause? Let us first start with what it is not. It is most assuredly not procrastination. Here, I know, voices will rise in protest: "Are you crazy? Everybody knows that procrastination, downright laziness, is the root of writer's block." This catchall word is probably the description of creative resistance most widely offered by writers. Procrastination is so eloquently evoked, so humorously described, so fervently cursed that surely any effort to overcome writer's block must involve pinning this monster of slothful inactivity to the mat by its allegorical opposite, Will Power, shouldn't it?

It should not. To believe so only reinforces the trap you are caught in. First of all, attributing your resistance to laziness is judging yourself with unwarranted harshness. Most practicing writers who suffer from writer's block are extremely hardworking, not to say compulsive, souls. For such a person to tell himself he is a lazy good-for-nothing is patently untrue, but this simple insult is easier to accept than trying to raise out of inner darkness the tangle of conflicting orders, counterorders, and outright mutiny raging in the bunker of his soul.

"Procrastinate," from the Latin *pro* ("forward") plus *crastinus* ("of tomorrow"), signifies literally "putting forward until tomorrow." Originally the term was descriptive, not judgmental, a neutral word meaning postponement. And even though procrastination now carries a pejorative connotation, it does not describe a motive. For a writer to say she procrastinates in no way explains *why* she does so. To say she doesn't write because she procrastinates is the same as saying she is sick because she doesn't feel well; it is a tautology, not a diagnosis. "Laziness" and "lack of self-discipline" are glosses supplied by the ever-obliging demon.

Placing the word in its proper perspective — namely, as just another way of saying "writer's block" — let us examine the true nature of procrastination. In common usage, it might best be described as a state of determined, though tortured, inactivity. Inactivity generally, like writer's block specifically, is usually viewed as a passive condition. But as Sartre tells us, inactivity is as clearcut an action as shooting skeet or flying to the moon; it represents the *decision* not to act. ("One must also decide to hesitate," the Polish aphorist Stanislaw Jerzy Lec has noted.) The highly active nature of procrastination becomes clear as we realize that it means *to push a task away from oneself.* Now a task cannot be pushed away unless it has first been put forward in some form or another, and here we come to the real nature of procrastination: it is a reaction.

But a reaction to what? Take note of what has already been said about writer's block: that it is a *healthy reaction of the organism to an inner state of imbalance.* The unconscious refusal to write is always based on sound principles — this truth cannot be repeated too often. Procrastination is no limp failure of will; it is an exasperated protest. When a writer announces to himself and to the world that he is a hopeless procrastinator, when he berates himself for inertia or lack of moral fiber, he is casting aspersions on his own deepest impulses.

Those who habitually describe themselves in this way might want to try a modest experiment. Divide a piece of paper into two columns. Write in the left column all the negative labels you apply to yourself during a period of creative resistance ("neurotic fraud," "spineless," "pathetic failure," and so on). In the right column put down all your positive self-descriptions as a writer. In comparing the columns, you may find it instructive to note two points: (1) the person described on the left and the person described on the right inhabit the same body; (2) there are often far fewer descriptive terms in the right-hand column than in the left. This indicates a failure in self-love, not in discipline. You are not a procrastinator. Your unconscious is trying to protect itself from further abuse in the only way it knows how: by shutting down communication.

In this way the seductive habit of self-hatred sets up a destructive division between the conscious personality and the (often) unconscious instincts, creating a permanent condition of war within the psyche that cannot be resolved unless both sides agree to lay down arms. *Getting* both sides to agree is the true task at hand in all cases of writer's block as well as in a good many other life events. Learning to manage this negotiation successfully is the complicated business of a lifetime.

Accomplishing this task is not nearly as easy as it sounds, because you will always be tempted to take the old familiar path in hopes of achieving the new healthy results. "Right," you say, "I will *stop* this neurotic self-hatred nonsense at once." But that is an ego command, and ego commands are not only doomed to failure in this situation, they are what got you into it in the first place. Resistance is almost never overcome forcibly; the application of force only hardens and entrenches it.

Thus it is equally a myth that "will power" is the sovereign cure for "procrastination." On the contrary, will power, representing as it does an ego command, is often the real villain. Lifting the block is by definition an effortless process; it does not involve the will. In the way of many old chestnuts, the story about the contest between the wind and the sun is illuminating here. Each wagered it could make a man take off his overcoat first. The wind blew fiercely, but the man only held his coat shut tighter. When the sun shone, he gladly took it off. This is the difference between attempting to exert will power on a recalcitrant unconscious and letting it bask in gentle acceptance.

The starting point for understanding why you procrastinate is to treat yourself with enough respect to assume that behind your inactivity lies an excellent, if not immediately apparent, reason. And this reason is to be found in an altogether different attitude or trait *inside yourself* that precipitated your procrastinating reaction. Why inside yourself? What about the backfiring cars, the booming stereo bass from the apartment next door, babies crying, phones ringing, malfunctioning computers, all the myriad other external distractions that so concern blocked writers and counselors helping blocked writers find the "right environment"?

If these factors were really significant to the writing experience, you would have to float in a sensory-deprivation tank to find total relief from outside stimuli. Moreover, once having created the "perfect environment," you are likely to find yourself still having major problems, as Proust did in his cork-lined bedchamber. Beyond a reasonable point, external irritations represent nothing more than a projection of internal conflict onto the world. They are rarely the causes of creative malaise. It is, in fact, the inner environment that badly needs some work and attention.

So we are back to the question: What is writer's block a reaction to? What is the unknown factor that provokes such a highly visible and aggravating response? The nature of the invisible stimulus can be partly deduced from the extremely emotional and hostile nature of the reaction. For however much you may want to see it as a kind of passive paralysis, procrastination, or writer's block, is a very aggressive act: it is a pushing away, a rejection.

What in particular is likely to have produced this repulsion within you? The nature of the writing you have set yourself to do? The severity of your deadline? The difficulty of turning extensive notes into a piece of prose? The unrealistic goals of perfection you aspire to? I will explore these specific issues later, but in most cases of chronic block it is not what you want to write, or deadlines, or any external hindrance that is stopping you. It is the *nature of the command to write.* How have you presented your desire to write to your unconscious self? Have you asked or have you ordered? Have you given him a choice of projects? Have you given him the flexibility to pick when, where, and how to write the project, or have you (having so little trust in yourself, your abilities, and your natural creative rhythm) screamed instead: "Get busy right this instant, or else!"

To this directive, the other part of you has only one response: "Forget it!"

Tragically, this stubborn rebellion by the unconscious usually triggers even more severe and desperate measures from you, its hapless guardian, to impose a strict regimen of work: total isolation, twelve-hour days, endless changes of locale and paraphernalia. But it is all for nothing. Attempts to be ruthless with yourself in order to "overcome procrastination" must always lead directly back to the hated condition itself, thereby engendering stalemate. Under these highly sensitized conditions even a reasonable order, *as long as it is an order,* will be rejected. The sense of failure and frustration increases exponentially as the vicious circle clicks back into gear.

People who accuse themselves of procrastination are not procrastinators. They are accusers. Far from being lazy, they are driven by such extremes of self-distrust and compulsive overcontrol that they throttle the spontaneous contact with self that all creative activity requires. The analogy with overeating is again apt: just as chronic overeaters are not typically fun-loving Falstaffian sensualists but starved creatures desperately and (let it be said) spitefully rebelling against the tyrant inside them who is ordering them to be thin, so procrastinators are not good-for-nothings but, as a rule, excessively conscientious strivers overwhelmed by their own demands.

What came first in this chicken-and-egg situation is unimportant. What matters, once the conflict has become an entrenched feature of your personality, is the dynamics of the control-rebellion impasse and how to get out of it. For if you see yourself as a procrastinator, you are suffering from a disease altogether different than laziness.

Let us now leave the bogus issue of procrastination and move to the real inner conflict it masks.

4

The Master-Slave Relationship

———— ❖ ————

All work and no play make Jack a dull boy.

IN STANLEY KUBRICK'S film of Stephen King's *The Shining* as adapted by Diane Johnson, this sentence, typed over and over, comprises the three-hundred-odd pages of manuscript the deranged writer Jack Torrance has pecked out in that classic last resort of blocked writers, a deserted mountain hotel. It is an eloquent telegram of protest from his enslaved unconscious. (Later Torrance takes an ax to his family, a less wholesome form of revolt.)

Works of art do require work to come into being. But unlike most of the jobs and chores that occupy our lives, the act of creating art involves the whole person. That is at once its great blessing and its curse. In the same way that clouds pass before and then uncover the sun, deep self-awareness is a state that comes and goes. The burden of imaginative writers is to be dependent much of the time on their level of self-awareness, for this state has an immediate effect on the ability to dream up something and put it down on paper. It is relatively easy, even desirable, to mow the lawn or balance a checkbook while on automatic pilot. But it is usually (though not always) very hard to write when not in a state of heightened awareness.

Then comes the doodling, the forcing, the lack of concentration, the guilt — all work and no play.

Being in touch with oneself is elusive and maddening, because it is a state that cannot be *controlled* but only *allowed*. Adjusting oneself to the demands of the unconscious, not the other way around, is the best way to "regulate" creativity. Of all the psychologies emerging in our era, the Gestaltists have paid the most attention to this problem of defusing ego control to allow for the spontaneous encounter with self. In the words of Fritz Perls:

> You don't drive a car according to a program like, "I want to drive 65 miles per hour." You drive according to the situation. You drive a different speed at night, you drive a different speed when there is traffic there, you drive differently when you are tired. You listen to the situation. The less confident we are in ourselves, the less we are in touch with ourselves and the world, the more we want to control.

"Listening to the situation" is something a tyrant, intent on asserting will at all costs, finds hard to do. Imposing on yourself an ego-conceived framework of duty, schedule, and appropriate topics of composition is an attempt to dam, channel, and otherwise divert the stream of spontaneous creation in directions it does not wish to follow and in which it would not naturally flow. This invariably triggers the unconscious reaction we call writer's block.

The creative experience can and must be guided, but it cannot be controlled. Control in its extreme form represents the attempt of one small segment of the psyche to declare absolute power over the rest. These strange fellow citizens of ours, as we all come painfully to realize in the course of a lifetime, are highly independent, egalitarian souls. They will not stand for any kind of dictatorship, and the forms their rebellion takes are as varied and devious as the human heart itself. Primary among these inner cotenants is that proud creature who likes to play. Every word a writer puts down is the product of a dialogue between the conscious self and the unconscious, and with every word the two move closer to fruitful partnership or war. If it comes to war, both sides will lose. If they cannot cooperate, they will destroy each other as well as their common undertaking.

You (here I address the conscious self, the side we all identify with) have the responsibility of guiding the spontaneous uprushings of the unconscious. But the minute you try to exert excessive control over the flow of unconscious ideas, the flow stops. You may get away with it in outside life, but within your heart that side of you *refuses* to be your slave. When this palace rebellion of the soul occurs, you have the choice of responding in one of several ways.

You may entrench yourself behind your bogus authority and issue an even stricter command, trying to compel obedience. "I said *create*, damn you! We'll sit here all day until you do it!" This overused response is not an option for chronically blocked writers, because they have typically abused the privilege of self-command with *too much* will. (In a milder form, however, this method does work for that small number of writers who have been gentle with themselves and rarely resort to barking out orders.)

The other, pleasanter option is to relax the will, unclench the muscles of your mind. You might take a walk, listen to music — then, if all parties agree, cautiously proceed with writing. Remember always to start with what you most *want* to write, as a hook to draw you into the process. Once you've gotten started, it's often not hard to shift course back to the project at hand.

If your resistance persists, you may be obliged to put aside the project for a longer period. Keeping your mind completely open and nonjudgmental, you can allow whatever doubts, hesitations, or other feelings you may be having about the work to enter consciousness. This may take days or weeks or even longer. Awareness of what is going wrong or right with your project takes its own time in emerging into consciousness, especially if you are not accustomed to listening to yourself. Such awareness will never break through at all if it encounters only a fortified stone wall.

The most desperate blocked writers should consider the back-door discipline of actively letting their fields lie fallow. Resolving entrenched writer's block often means having the courage to make a conscious decision not to write for a period of time. As long as that is happening anyway, why not risk a *positive* silence for a change? Dare to aim for less, and you will write more in the long run. Your long-term productivity will increase in direct proportion to the care and acceptance you lavish on your short-term silences.

Here is one way you might go about doing this. Make a decision not to do any creative work for a week or other definite time. Make this an active, positive choice that leaves you to enjoy all the rest of your life activities free from nagging guilt. The more energy you put into enjoying the state of not writing, the more successful this experiment will be. At the end of your week of nonwriting, take your pulse. Would you like to extend your grace period, or would you like to try some writing? Absolute honesty is essential here, for there is no "right" choice except the one you most incline toward. If you deeply prefer to have another week without writing, *give it to yourself* and enjoy it to the hilt. If you deeply prefer to start creative work, do so — but not on a production-quota basis.

At the end of your second week, test your true inclinations again — another week of the same (whichever it was), or is it time to switch? Again, either choice is right if you are basing your decision on what you truly want to do, not on what you *ought* to do. A set amount of time when you are actively not writing allows you to build momentum and anticipation toward doing some creative work.

Many blocked writers experience the week free of work as an enormous relief. To choose consciously not to work increases the sense of self-mastery and decreases self-blame, feelings of helplessness, and the like. Sincerely practiced, this exercise gradually helps blur the barriers between creating and noncreating until the week of creative work begins to feel like the holiday instead of the other way around.

In these calculated delays and postponements, which are actually one of the most vital parts of the creative process, may be recognized our *bête noire* procrastination in its true, transfigured form. A consciously taken rest period allows the unconscious either to let you know something is out of kilter in your approach or simply to proceed in various necessary but inaccessible activities that, though they lie outside your sphere of consciousness, will nonetheless allow the work in progress to carry on. What most chronically blocked writers lack is the gut faith in themselves that allows these needed intervals of silence to occur. Overcontrolling, self-distrustful personalities find the period of quiescence intolerable and interpret it as further proof of failure. For such writers the rest period may prove futile because their minds are closed off to the important information about the writing process or the nature of the project that the unconscious may be trying to communicate by temporarily halting the production of words.

Yet no work of art was ever completed without inscrutable pauses, unexplained hiatuses. The rewards of such deliberate procrastination, of complete and trusting surrender to the needs of that other side of the self, have been summed up by Eugène Delacroix: "When one yields oneself completely to one's soul, it opens itself completely to one."

OUGHT VERSUS WANT

The key symptom of the controlling personality is the *oughts* and *shoulds* that crowd his or her life. "I ought to go to exercise class." "I shouldn't eat chocolate again." "I should be able to write ten pages a day." If you were to make a list of all your most persistent *oughts* in life, you would probably note two striking characteristics of your list: the severity (often unrealistic) of the expectations, and the glaring, inescapable truth that the things you ought to do, you *don't*. The existential truth about oughts is that we don't do them. That's why they're oughts to begin with.

This is the classic dynamic of the master-slave relationship. Any command made by the ego that the unconscious finds unpalatable, it will not perform. Period. Almost anything we set up as an ought we are doomed never to accomplish. No matter how much the ego desires it, the rest of the psyche takes perverse pleasure in denying gratification. Though the master may stubbornly insist on staying the boss, the slave refuses to be the slave.

The Gestaltists characterized this personality conundrum as a split between two parts of the psyche characterized as the "topdog" and the "underdog." Here is Perls again:

> The topdog usually is righteous and authoritarian; he knows best. He is sometimes right, but always righteous. The topdog is a bully, and works with "You should" and "You should not." The topdog manipulates with demands and threats of catastrophe. . . .
>
> The underdog manipulates with being defensive, apologetic, wheedling, playing the cry-baby, and such. . . . The underdog is cunning, and usually gets the better of the topdog because the underdog is not as primitive as the topdog. So the topdog and underdog strive for control. Like every parent and child, they strive with each other for control. The person is fragmented into controller and controlled.
>
> This is the basis for the famous self-torture game. We usually take for granted that the topdog is right, and in many cases the topdog makes impossible perfectionistic demands. So if you are cursed with perfectionism, then you are absolutely sunk. This ideal is a yardstick which always gives you the opportunity to browbeat yourself, to berate yourself and others. Since this ideal is an impossibility, you can never live up to it.

I will return to the double-edged nature of perfectionism later. For now it's enough to note the distortion of perfectionism into a weapon we direct against our underdog unconscious self, who, as Perls points out, always wins in any inner conflict of this sort, though not in a productive way. By sabotaging orders, the slave becomes the true master. That is why we don't stick to our diets, exercise every day, or turn out ten pages of deathless prose like clockwork every morning. That other, unacknowledged side of ourselves prefers thumbing its nose — or, more accurately, cutting it off — to following orders.

Because it's so important to raise up the inner relationship from this level of hooligan brawling, you must begin to make a more conscious acquaintance with what lies within. One way to begin is to compose a completely spontaneous dialogue between your conscious self ("I") and your unconscious (give it a separate identity and name, or let one emerge from the dialogue). When you finish your dialogue, describe the personalities of the two speakers. What kind of person is the "I"? What kind of person is the unconscious? (Individuals are highly variable; you may find creatures other than topdogs and underdogs.) Are they opposites, or are they kindred spirits? Are they at loggerheads, or do they achieve resolution? (Don't try to force a resolution; that is your ego taking charge. Be absolutely honest about where you are at the moment.) You might consider rewriting this dialogue whenever you experience a new resistance, as a way of focusing on exactly what about the project is bothering your other side at a given time.

But, some will still argue, goals like exercising or dieting or writing ten pages a day are modest, healthy ones to aim for. They are not examples of impossible perfectionism; they lie easily within the realm of human achievement. *Other* people achieve these goals, certainly; the world is full of slender people, athletic people, prolific writers. Yes, because most of these people (masochistic overachievers excluded) do what they do by preference, not command. They *like* to exercise, for example, and it fits their natural rhythm; no unnatural effort is required. But chances are that these same well-exercised people are tormenting themselves for not doing enough of something else — reading, for example — that the exercise-blocked individual feels not a shred of resistance to doing. These other people believe that reading is a wholesome, self-improving activity they would do a great deal more of were they not so spineless and undisciplined.

Behind the word "ought," then, lies a hideous tangle of autocratic attitudes and superstitions that can strangle the joy of writing. These are some standard oughts the demon puts into the beginning writer's mind: (1) If I'm ever going to be famous, I ought to be writing a lot more than I do. (2) I ought to write like (pick any well-known writer) Ernest Hemingway did, up before daybreak, standing at his desk, always stopping when he still knew what would happen next so he'd have a starting place the next day. (3) I ought to be writing every night and weekend instead of using this time to relax.

It is easy, once they are dragged into the daylight of consciousness, to counter each of these assumptions. First, you can only write to write, not to be famous. Expectations of future glory extinguish creativity. As for following the Master's Example, his first two bits of wisdom are almost certainly major embellishments of the truth, and I suspect the last one is, too — Hemingway, for most of his later writing life, was severely blocked by alcoholism. Even if it were all true, though, beware always the fallacy of modeling yourself after a famous author. Every writer, by heeding her own deepest instincts, spins a unique web of idiosyncratic habits that make up a writing routine. At best, it's helpful to know there's so much individual variation. But what worked for Kafka is not necessarily going to work for you.

As for the third ought, do not use writing as an excuse to ruin your life.

Now if writing itself is on a writer's list of oughts, this does not necessarily mean — especially if she has already written a great deal — that her ego has shoehorned her into a profession for which she has no great desire or avocation. What it probably indicates is that over the years she has moved away from her initial childlike and playful joy in writing. It is now a duty-bound and ego-ridden chore. And no activity, viewed from this perspective, is very enticing.

Think of a project you have been struggling to write, with no success. Make a list of thoughts about the project, beginning each item on the list in the following manner:

1. I *ought* to write X because . . .

Now write a new list:

1. I *refuse* to write X because . . .

Notice that your inability to get into your project means that your second list of reasons is more powerful than your first. Can you learn to value your refusals consciously as much as you do unconsciously — that is, take them seriously enough to *act* on them instead of trying to steamroll over them?

Now write a third list:

1. I would *love* to write X.

List everything you would feel eager and enthusiastic about starting, no matter how trivial or silly your ego judges them to be. And you might consider trying one of these items, just for the fun of it.

One way that even experienced writers get caught in the "ought/refuse" conflict without considering the easy "love and prefer" solution is by overidentifying with an image of themselves as a certain kind of author, usually of the "serious" variety. The phoniness of this image is enough by itself to cause a temporary or permanent shutdown of creative powers, but it often leads to the further error of choosing writing projects geared to the image instead of to deep preference. It is one of the pervasive ironies of the creative life that integrity often operates only on the unconscious level, as a writer's block.

Most writers who have struggled through the beginning and intermediate stages of their apprenticeship have had at least some of this inflation knocked out of them by the enormous amounts of rejection and frustration they have had to endure. During the long struggle to gain a regular writing rhythm, they are more likely to find they have reached for the brass ring of discipline but have grasped instead the nettle of control.

DISCIPLINE AND CONTROL

I have already stressed that creative discipline is based on spontaneous, pleasurable play, not a Spartan regime of stern self-control. From the Latin *disciplina,* meaning instruction or knowledge (a disciple is literally a "learner"), discipline is training that produces a certain pattern of behavior. The grim connotation the word has come to carry reflects the austerity of our culture rather than the true nature of this enjoyable, life-enhancing experience. Discipline is not the same as forcing oneself to do distasteful tasks. Tasks, in fact, tend to become distasteful only to the degree to which they are forced. That we usually mistake control for discipline is a measure of our personal as well as societal rigidity. Only a writing routine that has the consent of the total psyche can provide a foundation solid enough to sustain a writer through the years of drudgery and tedium all creative effort requires.

How does one free discipline from the killing grip of control? Here is the therapist Muriel Schiffman's solution:

> I used to struggle anew each day with the problem, "Should I write now or later, or maybe skip this one day?" until I began to treat myself exactly as I did my small children.
>
> Now at a specific hour each morning I stop whatever I am doing and sit down at the typewriter. No need for the daily conflict between "want" and "should." . . . I write for exactly one hour each morning, no more, no less. Writing for one hour seems a natural creative activity for me. Ideas flow smoothly without stress or strain. But after an hour the work becomes an effort of will, a forced assignment, performed with much physical tension (clenched teeth, etc.), like swimming upstream.
>
> I learned by trial and error that morning is the best time for me to write: words come easily. Later in the day I get bogged down in a compulsive search for the "perfect" word. I torture myself with inhibiting thoughts. . . .
>
> I do not *know* why this happens in the afternoon and not in the morning. . . . My Adult self avoids frustrating the Child in

me by choosing a time which is most comfortable for writing, just as it chooses the most satisfying menu when I diet. I never forced my children to eat foods they disliked just because they were "good" for them.

Schiffman established her discipline by trusting the organism, not her ego. She guided herself only to the extent of setting aside that hour to allow the writing to happen; that was her conscious self's productive input in this partnership. Her trust in her innate creative rhythms (instead of the judgmental "Only *one* hour?") was rewarded by a free and uninterrupted flow of writing for the allotted period every day. And an hour a day can produce a lot of writing.

Here the Devil may tempt you with the thought: "If I do this much in an hour, think how much I could do if I worked eight hours every day!" This kind of falsely rational conclusion will only get you into trouble. Most blocked writers have a conscious expectation of results that far exceeds their unconscious preference, and the "block" is nothing more than the gap between these two opposing perspectives. The nature of your deep inner inclinations, their rhythms and direction, can be determined only by patiently *allowing* a pattern to emerge. Once the pattern has surfaced, your conscious self can step in cautiously to guide it, exploit it, and build on it. Each time you attempt to work faster than your inner rhythm, it will break down. That is your signal to let up and allow the unconscious once again to set the pace. You determine your limits by testing them gently but repeatedly, then respecting them — no matter how unlike anybody else's they are.

This can be a time-consuming process, even for a person who does not tend to be overcontrolling. For the blocked writer who has spent years mistreating himself in a master-slave struggle, it is likely to take even longer. Freedom to develop a true discipline does not come overnight. The abused organism needs time to heal its wounds, to recover from the all too familiar pattern of command-rebellion-punishment and to begin to establish a new one. Such a gentle reorganization can indeed occur. And it is a far pleasanter process than whipping oneself. The key is to be able to give up pain for pleasure, and most people find this very hard to do.

Donald Newlove, a fiction writer and recovered alcoholic, recounts the agonies he experienced when he was blocked by ambitious plans for a nine-hundred-page novel:

> For three months I sat around my fellowship table [at Alcoholics Anonymous meetings] and complained of my fears and paralysis. . . . I'd explain carefully that my method of writing was to write a first draft in longhand, type that up, correct and retype it from start to finish, then again correct and totally retype it. Since the novel was set at NINE HUNDRED PAGES, this meant that when done I'd have filled THIRTY-SIX HUNDRED PAGES with my writing. This was daunting. The idea that I would have to fill 3600 pages with my imagination was now a black mountain of work that had kept me stoned with weakness for three months.

Then came the epiphany:

> This dumb phrase suddenly filled me with light. It was: One Day at a Time. . . . To write it I had only to write one word at a time, one phrase at a time, one sentence at a time, one paragraph at a time, one page at a time, one day at a time — and if I wrote four pages a day I'd be done in three years. The magnitude of the results of this simpleminded approach to boating my white whale sent me home like a shot after the meeting and I jumped at the dining room table with a blank sheet and began.

What Newlove describes is the conversion experience of a man who stopped wanting to punish himself and started wanting to be kind to himself. It is perhaps significant that this change occurred in a therapeutic setting.

To gain true discipline, it is necessary to learn to treat yourself with at least the same courtesy, respect, and affection you accord your spouse, friends, and even the grocery store bagger. This sounds easy, but it is not. The urge to hate and tyrannize yourself does not go away by itself; *real* effort is required to dispel it. Even in fairy tales, frogs don't change back into princes until a ritual period of time (a year and a day, seven years) has passed and certain tasks have been performed. We have already seen the importance of time; the task of gaining self-respect is a lifework.

And there is one thing always to remember. The long-afflicted writer who suddenly feels the joy of a spontaneous flow of words wants to say at once, "That's it! I'm cured. I'll never have writer's block again." But all you have done is reap the benefits of a friendly dialogue, instead of a hostile engagement, with your resistance. As an essential part of the creative process, the resistance was, is, and will be a constant; the only thing that has changed is your attitude toward it. Without resistance one can do nothing.

RESPECTING THE EGO

In these pages you will frequently find a villainous, punishing ego contrasted with a noble, put-upon unconscious. The distorted emphasis is necessary to right the balance between these two components of the psyche in writers who experience a block. Such writers have habitually attempted to dominate their unconscious instead of establishing a true relationship with it. Art, as Cocteau said, is a "marriage of the conscious and the unconscious"; it does not spring from an unequal relationship. Finding ways of relaxing the iron grip on self is the main purpose of this book, which suggests that the path back to writing is, by definition, free of effort.

Once the imbalance is righted, however, we must recognize that the ego is obviously a powerful player in the writing process whose important function is to guide and structure the inchoate outpourings of the unconscious. The unconscious, in turn, is by no means always the "better half" of this duo; unregulated, it can sweep a person into a crushing depression or even psychosis. There is sometimes a fine line between the spontaneous desires of the playful child and the infantile destructiveness of some unconscious impulses. The crucial issue here is restoring the natural equilibrium of these forces.

Sometimes — blocked writers be wary here — the only way out of an impasse is to exert the ego, not the unconscious. As Christopher Isherwood noted, "Even the tiniest act of the will towards a thing is better than not doing it at all." And tiny acts of will, as we shall see, get you where you want to go much more efficiently than great big acts of will that are hollow and unsupported by desire. Contrary to stereotype, art lives in the modest effort, not the grandiose one.

The last word on successfully exerting an act of will against resistance should go, by way of contrast, to a highly prolific writer, Joyce Carol Oates:

> One must be pitiless about this matter of "mood." In a sense, the writing will *create* the mood. . . . Generally I've found this to be true: I have forced myself to begin writing when I've been utterly exhausted, when I've felt my soul as thin as a playing card, when nothing has seemed worth enduring for another five minutes . . . and somehow the activity of writing changes everything.

To use the act of writing itself to cancel out resistance and render it irrelevant is a powerful strategy, and one that fluent writers employ as a matter of course. To use this strategy exclusively, however, is to risk missing the important messages, personal and aesthetic, that certain resistances may be trying to communicate. Think twice about burying your friend the block — even when you have the shovelful of words to do it — before you listen to what he has to say.

5
Perfectionism and Criticism

——— ❖ ———

The perfectionists . . . finding or believing life to be intolerable
except for art's perfection, by the very violence of their homage
can render art imperfect.

— CYRIL CONNOLLY

T HE QUEST for perfection in art is the heroic attempt to
achieve total mastery over one's materials, to bring the
work of art to its fullest state of completion. In the ideology of
the inner kingdom, "perfectionism" is a positive factor in the
creative process; it acts as a real spur to artistic achievement
and is one of the vital ingredients that raises art above self-
expression. Without the slightly obsessive, controlling urge to
excel, artists lack that fine cutting edge, that need to *make
complete* (the literal meaning of "perfect") which produces all
real works of art.

To be a perfectionist as a writer is therefore a necessary
virtue, a blessing even. Writers should not stand the master-
slave relationship on its head and scold themselves for a desire
to be perfect in their writing. The impulse to perfect, like the
impulse to postpone, is a natural part of the creative process.

Past a certain point of healthy obsession, however, the im-

petus to shape and perfect reverses itself and becomes negative. You know you have crossed the border from persistence
into paralysis when every fragile word or idea withers under
the glare of disapproval and faultfinding from your demonic
interiorized judge and executioner, the insidious voice that
whispers that your best is not only not good enough but is
awful, worthless, ridiculous. This is the moment when the
blessing becomes the curse.

Here again you will usually find that will power ("the power
of positive thinking") is a pitifully weak defense in the face of
this judge's relentless ferocity. Pumping yourself up with
phony defensive compliments ("But I *am* a good writer") is
exhausting and not much help, either. After a token bit of
resistance to this onslaught of insults, you may collapse into
grim and acquiescent silence. In this case, writer's block functions as an automatic survival mechanism geared to protect you
from an avalanche of outrageously punitive self-judgments.
Unless you can find a way to soften that inner critical voice
which is your own, it literally isn't *safe* to write, for no sane
person voluntarily subjects herself to this kind of abuse. Your
writer's block will continue to protect you from your self-
hatred until you find a way, not to bulldoze through the block,
but to defuse the hatred. But how, exactly, is this to be done?

Before we examine the possibilities, two interesting varia-
tions on the perfectionist phenomenon need to be mentioned.
One of these might be termed "fear of perfection" — that is,
breaking off in the middle of your effort because you have
started so well, so flawlessly that you fear (no, you *know*) you
are incapable of carrying the whole thing off at the same level.
A friend and colleague, William Searle, recalls how, as a first
grader in 1943 during the height of World War II, he and his
classmates obsessively drew military airplanes. The rules regarding identification of these planes were strict: handsome
airplanes were American; "scrubby and mean-looking" planes
were German or Japanese and were generally set on fire as an
added touch. These conventions posed a real aesthetic chal-

lenge, because it was harder to bring off an American plane successfully and, as Searle notes, "flames had the advantage of being comparatively easy to draw." Ultimately one of his classmates found himself in a classic dilemma:

> Though relatively untalented, he had managed by a fluke to draw the nose, wings, and most of the fuselage of as beautiful an aircraft as I had ever seen. . . . It was too large, sleek and elegant-looking to be anything convincingly but American — there was nothing for it but to draw stars. Should he try to finish it at the risk of spoiling it? or set it on fire?

Searle's classmate chose the easy way out. Instead of finishing it, he torched the American airplane, a decision that outraged his fellow students as much for aesthetic reasons as for patriotic ones.

My own sympathies go entirely with that first grader who, through no fault of his own, was suddenly launched down the inexorable and unforgiving road of perfectionism. So what if he committed a sin against Art? Anyone who has ever set fire to a story or poem out of sheer failure of nerve can fully appreciate his point of view. The spectacle of naked excellence can be frightening, even repelling, and one's strongest impulse is sometimes to say, "Torch it, for God's sake!" On this principle Moslem weavers always include a deliberate error in the pattern of their rugs to avoid offense in the sight of God, the only entity able to encompass perfection. The poet Robert Graves recast this pious sentiment as follows: "A perfect poem is impossible. Once it had been written, the world would end."

For literary history's most famous case of a work immolated in midcomposition, we must turn to Samuel Taylor Coleridge's poem "Kubla Khan." His transparent excuse of a "person from Porlock" who happened to interrupt the sacred trance of poetic concentration, together with the cynical responses of later poets, is a major document in the annals of writer's block. See the Appendix.

Imperfection, finally, has its own inscrutable advantages. The English novelist Penelope Farmer tells the story of a school competition for the best picture of a party. The prize-winning drawing showed an empty room, a table piled high with festive goodies and, in the background, a single hand emerging from behind a door standing slightly ajar. Asked about her inspiration for this magnificently evocative scene, the child artist replied that she had to do it that way because she couldn't draw people.

After fear of perfection, the second variant of the perfectionist block might be called the "reverse Midas effect." This happens after the writer has finished a preliminary draft and rereads it only to discover that an amazing transformation has occurred: what seemed to be pure gold during the throes of composition has turned into something brown and odorous. The resulting effect on the writer's pride is so devastating that he either throws the work away or embarks on an ill-advised course of drastic and often fatal revision. Curiously, a third reading of the offending piece can turn it into something neither good nor bad but merely completed. It is therefore important to remember that all writers are notoriously inconstant in their attitudes toward their work; the value they accord any given work will shift and change from moment to moment like the weather. A "final" judgment is virtually impossible to reach, and for many reasons this is a good thing.

In all versions of the block writers unconsciously erect to combat excessive perfectionism, it is clear that habitual and severe faultfinding is a problem of the personality, the whole human being, not of artistic technique. Carrying perfectionism beyond its clear function to "make complete" into a realm of unending negative judgment is self-hatred in still another disguise. Yet judgment, in the form of criticism, is an ongoing event in the life of every writer. How can criticism, the self-administered kind as well as that rendered by others, be tempered into the guide it was meant to be so that it does not become a silencing gag?

SELF-CRITICISM

Perhaps in order to write a really great book, you *must* be rather
unaware of the fact. You can slave away at it and change every
adjective to some other adjective, but perhaps you can write
better if you leave the mistakes.

— JORGE LUIS BORGES

Criticism, first of all, was designed to take place *after* composition, not during it. An artist who discovers another person —
the critic — hanging over her shoulder and giving the thumbs-
up or thumbs-down sign to every brush stroke would be entitled to commit homicide. Nothing is so distracting, during the
heat of creation, as the carping, niggling, nitpicking voice of
critical judgment. If, when a writer is furiously composing, a
voice interrupts out of nowhere and says, "Stop! What you just
wrote stinks!" the natural response is to stop and reread. Still
partly in the blessed trance of creation (in which all judgment
is suspended), he can see nothing the matter with what he
wrote. Whereupon the critical faculty announces smugly, "You
wrote, 'on the table in the back room.' Don't put two prepositional phrases in a row like that. Don't you know any better?"
Caught up short, the writer meekly acquiesces: "Oh, dear, let
me see . . . 'He put the cards on the back room table.' No.
'Going into the back room, he put the cards —' " By now his
concentration and train of thought have vanished and heaven
is truly lost.

Some writers compose in such a way that they cannot proceed to the next word until the word under consideration is
exactly as it should be. In their case, self-criticism is no obsta-
cle but part of a tried-and-true modus operandi; they are completely adapted to its presence. For other writers, this carping
voice interrupts spontaneous performance, tripping them in
midstride; if mistakenly heeded, it can effectively shut down a
day's work. For these writers self-criticism has no place in
first-draft composition, and a better response to the intrusive

complaint about prepositional phrases would be, "Shut up. I'll take care of that *if* I think it needs taking care of, when I rewrite. Quit interrupting."

Notice that this interaction is slightly different from the one that governs the master-slave relationship underlying most chronic writer's block. In the case of chronic intrusive self-criticism your unconscious negativity is the master and your conscious self is the slave; your own self-contempt is acting upon you almost as an impersonal force. This entrenched and automatic negativity poses a serious danger that demands reverse tactics. Far from being "relaxed into," self-insult must be stopped at the source: you have to face the bully down. This time the ego, the beleaguered slave, must overthrow the invisible tyrant; you must refuse to accept those lies. When the voice begins, you must tell it in no uncertain terms to stop. It will know perfectly well whether you are bluffing.

How do you say no with conviction to the bully? How do you summon the authority? There are many excellent reasons to do so, of course — for example, that obsessive self-criticism is stifling, life denying, and ultimately a dull and unadventuresome method of self-laceration. This sort of intellectualizing makes little impression on the street mugger inside you. The only way to put conviction in your voice is to realize that you are facing a life-or-death situation. Encountering your self-hatred is potentially as dangerous as being accosted by a crazed gunman, a special kind of madman who will spare you if you oppose him but will almost certainly kill you if you give in. To cave in to excessive self-criticism, to surrender yourself along with all you have struggled so hard to create, is to allow your personhood to be violated at the deepest level. Over a lifetime, unfortunately, such a series of meek surrenders can become an addictive habit.

To say no to self-denigration involves a commitment of the whole spirit to believe in yourself and to take seriously what you are doing. It cannot be a shallow behavior-modification exercise in which — as that peculiar brand of psychological theorizing goes — if I say the magic words "I believe in me" enough times, they come true. The writer must believe in himself completely *before* he can say these words with sufficient strength to silence the torrent of abuse.

Silencing self-criticism when it exceeds its natural limits does not mean that everything you write will be wonderful or that someday you will not pick up something you wrote and discover that it really was trite and worthless after all. The act of writing does not in itself guarantee the production of art. All you are really doing is buying time and freedom — to write first, perfect later.

There is still another critic to deal with, one no writer is equipped to face until he has managed to come to terms with the enemy within. This new critic is the writer's audience: every soul out there who reads his work and feels compelled to comment on it.

CRITICISM BY OTHERS

Most writers, in the course of their careers, become thick-skinned and learn to accept vituperation, which in any other profession would be unimaginably offensive, as a healthy counterpoise to praise.

— EVELYN WAUGH

Unlike the writer himself, whose self-criticisms must always be subjective, readers are potentially capable of taking a truly disinterested dislike to his work. Their lack of enthusiasm has an objective existence that cannot be commanded away by an act of faith in oneself. As a writer you are obliged to live with scorn and rejection as well as with praise, which can equally cause problems of its own.

Criticism of your work by others is likely to have one of two undesirable effects: it will inflate you if it is favorable, or it will deflate you if it is unfavorable. Neither condition is suitable for writing, and each can take a toll on your work. This is as true of a well-known author reading a bad (or good) review in a national journal as it is of the beginner showing a first effort to a college roommate.

The unpredictable and unsettling reactions of others begin the moment you hand an unpublished manuscript to another person. At this time it is wise to bear a couple of things in mind. First, manuscript reading is an art apart from ordinary reading. Unless the person to whom you have given your work is an experienced and sensitive reader or fellow writer, your typed page will lack for him the authority of the printed page. For most people outside the writing world a typescript is an unfamiliar reading medium that also spells "amateur"; they tend to find flaws in it they wouldn't perceive in the same piece if it were published in a venue they recognized and respected. Conversely, for many professional writers who have toiled too long in the trenches of creative writing programs, the same pile of pages looks about as inviting as first prize in the apple-pie-eating contest: they have read too many manuscripts.

Second, whether your reader is a fellow writer or a friend, there is always the important question of taste. Not all people like the same things, nor do they like them for the same reasons. Above a certain level of technical competence, one person's Shakespeare is another's hack; you begin to realize this only after a great many people have read and commented on your work. Some people will like your work even if it is very bad; others will hate it even if it is very good. Someone can be utterly wrong about your work but heartbreakingly persuasive in his reasons; a completely inarticulate person may intuitively sense what your work is all about.

This is the maddening, elusive nature of criticism. We want it to be an absolute, and it is not. It never is. How are valid criticisms to be distinguished from invalid ones? Determining whether a judgment of your work has merit and what, if anything, you can do about it is one of the most difficult tasks of the writing experience. In fact, it is often impossible. We are as blind to most of the effects our works have on others as we are to the impression our personalities make. For the thousand ways to rationalize away someone's negative reception of our work, there is the single haunting (and usually far more compelling) possibility that the critic may be right on target.

In the end, writers need to rely on their own deepest inner convictions about their work. Does the information you are receiving from the outside resonate with what you are feeling inside? If so, it may be worth doing something about. Tuning in to relevant criticism and tuning out the irrelevant becomes a delicate matter of sorting the seeds, slowly and painstakingly. Needless to say, this fine task of discrimination is virtually impossible to accomplish if a domineering inner critic is constantly running radio interference or agreeing eagerly with the worst criticism.

If you are wincing under the sting of negative feedback from others, an unconscious block will rise up between you and your writing as a radical measure to shield you from further abuse — if you don't write anything at all, you can't be criticized. When your wounds have healed sufficiently, you will probably be able to continue. Those who are almost permanently crippled after reading a bad review must ask themselves why. Have they allowed the voice of their critic to form an unholy chorus with their own internal demon, thereby providing a spurious justification for self-hatred?

Given the high vulnerability of most writers, should you show your work to anyone at all besides those responsible for getting it published? This depends entirely on you and your assessment of how defenseless you really are. Most artists of all kinds have a strong show-off impulse when a work is done, a kind of grand, promiscuous self-display that tends to blind them temporarily to the fact that not everyone is going to love the piece as much as they do. "Writers have a little holy light within, like a pilot light, which fear is always blowing out," Cynthia Ozick has stated. "When a writer brings a manuscript fresh from the making, at the moment of greatest vulnerability, that's the moment for friends to help get the little holy light lit again."

The encouragement of friends or other writers may help create a benign, accepting environment in which your writing can flourish — if you are clever enough to find readers who always like your work. Beware of the beginner's error of assuming that just because your reader is another writer, he or she will be sympathetic to your intentions. In many cases the reverse is true: writers who are passionately attached to their own ways of rendering art may be far less objective or insightful than other readers.

Protect yourself, then, or expose yourself, in the way your instinct feels is right. You will have to determine by trial and considerable error whether this means showing work to anyone who will read it or showing it only to those you want to publish it. If you are just starting out and feel tentative, it is perfectly acceptable to spend years accreting your work in the dark; many writers begin in this way. But it is a big mean world out there, and farther down the road a case can be made (if you are ready for it) for the tempering effects of rejection and adverse criticism on your own nature as well as on your work. As we like to say about any thoroughly unpleasant experience, it builds character. For how can you distinguish valid negative criticism from invalid if you have never experienced either? You are likely to be crushed by the latter, when it inevitably comes, if you have not had some experience of different reactions and have learned how to define yourself independent of them.

A useful exercise for writers who feel excessively vulnerable to the words of critics is to one-up the opposition by writing your own evaluation ahead of time. If your work is about to be published or critiqued, take some time to write a review of your own, in the third person (to distance yourself). As if you were an objective reviewer, explain the purpose or intent of the work and, most important, its strongest and weakest features. Be as detailed as you can, and be honest in your evaluation.

You now have a document against which to compare the reactions of others. If a certain editor does not like the work, you do not have to identify wholly with her criticisms; you have already defined your own position as distinct from hers. Some of this editor's strictures you may want to accept; others, reject. Some will come as a complete surprise; others may be identical to your own. With your own review on paper (as opposed to in your head, where it is not nearly so authoritative), you are at least able to keep her viewpoint separate from yours. Conversely, if a certain critic finds you the absolute greatest, your recorded observations about your work can help keep you from experiencing a dangerous inflation.

THE PERILS OF PRAISE

The wrong kind of praise can be as lethal as a pan. This is a point that needs some emphasis. Praise, which we naturally (but mistakenly) feel no need to defend ourselves against, can be just as insidious as rejection, and is no more likely to be true. Its inflationary effects can remove you as far from your real self as a bad notice can. Unlike bad press, however, praise is something you can rapidly become dependent on. When fickle tastes inevitably change, the previously cosseted writer is likely to be more devastated than the poor soul who has continued to struggle along under steady fire or against sheer indifference. If you rely on praise to keep afloat, what happens when critics decide you're no good? You may go down with the ship. When the English writer Barbara Pym's eighth novel was inexplicably turned down by the publisher of her first seven, she was unable to write for the next sixteen years. This sensitive writer accepted and internalized a shortsighted "market" decision as an absolute judgment of her worth.

It is a truism of creative endeavor that praise in the early stages is always beneficial. The poet Diane Wakoski, however, makes an interesting case against automatic approval, especially in the setting that has become the traditional launching pad of young American writers, the creative writing class:

The workshop system produces what I call workshop junkies: people who do not become original writers because they continue to be encouraged for everything they do. They get so used to and so needful of that encouragement that they never want to go out in the world and struggle with that feeling of aloneness: "No one ever reads me. What does my work mean? I've written for fifty years and it hasn't done anything to change the world." Or, "I've spent all my time doing this and I'm not even satisfied with it." Those are all the feelings that even a great writer has. . . . The workshop . . . allows [the student] to think that he's already a poet before he's even written 15 or 50 or 150 poems.

In too large doses, praise can have a paralyzing effect on your work in the form of a block: a piece that has garnered accolades can become an impossibly hard act to follow. Overpraise of a young writer's first novel and her corresponding inflation can combine to produce an inhibiting environment for further creative efforts. A writer in this all too common position who is starting a new work must make a strenuous effort to return, in spirit, to the lost Eden of obscurity — a region in which the innocent and uncorrupted unconscious prefers to perform its playful acts of art.

Before or after publication, letting the opinions of others define your work gives them far too much power over your artistic identity. Paradoxically, lack of interest in or outright dislike of your writing, if you can keep it from overwhelming you, may work more to your advantage than an uncritically enthusiastic reception. Benign neglect can give you the freedom to grow as a writer; outright disapproval, if you survive it (as all writers must, at some point in their careers), can temper you as a person, giving your inner self a Zen-like equilibrium that remains unchanged in the face of good fortune or bad.

FINDING A MIDDLE GROUND

The real problem is that all of us tend to identify, to merge automatically, with criticism of our work that is intelligently expressed. In a nanosecond the critical words traverse the small distance from the printed page to the bottom of our souls, where they rankle for all eternity.

This internalization of criticism can exert a great influence on the direction your writing takes in style, voice, and genre. It can also engender the most horrific writing blocks as you attempt to assimilate it. In the desire to improve and perfect your craft, you will find it almost impossible to resist the guidance offered by others, yet by taking this advice you run the risk of twisting yourself out of shape. The effect of even laudatory remarks is often to throw you off center and out of touch with your own writerly instincts. And if a barrage of negative comments has greeted your latest effort, do you flatly decide it is totally undeserved (arrogant approach) or totally deserved (craven approach)?

The healthiest reaction available to a writer probably leans in the direction of "in your face." Philip Larkin had his own cautionary tale on this problem, and a suitable response: "You remember Tennyson reading an unpublished poem to Jowett; when he had finished, Jowett said, 'I shouldn't publish that if I were you, Tennyson.' Tennyson replied, 'If it comes to that, Master, the sherry you gave us at lunch was downright filthy.'" And here is Cynthia Ozick: "I was taking a course with Lionel Trilling and wrote a paper for him with an opening sentence that contained a parenthesis. He returned the paper with a wounding reprimand: 'Never, never begin an essay with a parenthesis in the first sentence.' Ever since then, I've made a point of starting out with a parenthesis in the first sentence."

On the most important issues, the truth probably lies somewhere between a critic's carping judgment and one's own outraged sense of honor. But it is difficult to tolerate the uncertainties. How much easier to declare yourself all the way on one side or the other, thereby closing out crippling doubt!

If you shut out criticism entirely, however, you are losing a chance to grow and to understand more deeply (though probably never fully) the impression your works make on others.

On the other hand, if you accept every comment about your work as gospel, you are heading for worse trouble. "I will *not* write that bad way anymore that nobody likes! I will write the way that has been recommended to me by my betters and be a good boy/girl.' A vow like this is guaranteed to trigger a rebellion in your psyche. Either you experience a severe block or, writing according to others' expectations, you depart from your own need to experiment and your writing develops a glossy, false veneer. This development can occur in all sorts of ways that seem relatively benign at first.

To stand the middle ground between these two extremes is the most difficult task of all — to be able to entertain the contradictory possibilities that your writing may be terrible or great or somewhere in between. But this open-minded position is most likely to keep your conscious and unconscious selves in steady dialogue. Whether you possess the strength to do this without losing your balance depends on how carefully you have cultivated that inner instinct Rilke called conscience:

> In artistic work one needs nothing so much as conscience: it is the sole standard. (Criticism is not one, and even the approval or rejection of others active outside of criticism should only very seldom, under unmistakable conditions, acquire influence.) That is why it is very important not to misuse one's conscience in [one's] early years, not to become hard at the place where it lies. It must remain light through everything; one may feel it just as little as any inner organ that is withdrawn from our will. The gentlest pressure emanating from it, however, one must heed, else the scale on which one will later have to test every word of the verses to be written will lose its extreme sensitivity.

If you have not learned how to listen consciously to this internal guide, or if you simply refuse to pay any attention to it, writer's block often intervenes as an unconscious and involuntary ethical self-regulator.

If you can balance criticism with at least the rudiments of

self-belief, in time this inner resilience will gradually supplant the more primitive mechanism of writer's block as the protector of your selfhood and the integrity of your work. Then self-criticism and criticism by others will serve their proper function, as guides pointing out a direction that you, the final judge and arbiter, may or may not choose to follow, according to your deepest preference.

6

Excessive Ambition

———— ❖ ————

[Ross Lockridge] talked about his book without a pause. He
explained that he and William Shakespeare had solved a particular dramatic problem in the same fashion and guessed that in
two hundred years' time readers would still be discussing the
symbolism of *Raintree County*. His amazed audience looked for
some sign of jest, or the chance to join the conversation, in vain.
— JOHN LEGGETT
Ross and Tom

T HE TRAGEDY of a now almost forgotten young author
like Lockridge — who, unable to begin a new book
and plagued by severe depression, took his own life shortly
after the publication of *Raintree County* — is not his audac-
ity in comparing his own work to Shakespeare's, but his obsessive need to derive a sense of worth from it. An artist is
likely to undervalue himself to the same degree that he over-
values, or overinvests himself in, his work. And once the work
begins to carry this extra burden of compensation for extreme feelings of inferiority, the unconscious partner begins
to balk.

There is an almost mathematical ratio between soaring,
grandiose ambition, when it is not firmly anchored in the daily
trivia of production, and a severe creative block. Norman

Mailer, in the years when he declared that he would "try to hit the longest ball ever to go up into the accelerated air of our American letters," was unable to write fiction at all. The melodramas he settled down to produce in later middle age are not, one suspects, the work originally announced — though the author periodically issued bulletins of its imminent appearance for thirty years after making his proud boast. Meanwhile, in an amazing case of literary synchronicity, Harold Brodkey (who once declared, "It's dangerous to be as good a writer as I") modestly explained to a reporter that it took him those same thirty years (1961 to 1991, give or take a year) to write a long-anticipated novel because of his reluctance to be anointed as, "if some of the people who talk to me are right, well . . . possibly not only the best living writer in English, but someone who could be the rough equivalent of a Wordsworth or a Milton."

One might expect overambition to be a beginner's problem, adolescent daydreaming of the sort everyone loves to indulge in at the start of an endeavor, the kind that drops away after years of humbling labor when writers realize what an enormous amount of work (not merely that overrated commodity, talent) stands between them and Tolstoy's achievements. But this is not the case. Inflation is an ongoing psychological problem for many writers. There are countless well-known authors whose lust for greatness throbs in every line, ruining the natural grace of their work with the self-consciousness that comes from pathological ambition — and not coincidentally, these writers are also often severely blocked.

Still, fantasies of grandeur are most likely to form when a writer's mode of self-expression is not yet clearly defined and all things — too many things — seem possible. The achievement of past literary giants can certainly serve as inspiration, but to reach those snowy peaks in the distance requires decades of painfully slow backpacking, one foot after the other. And each writer who gets to the end of her trail, wherever that happens to be, will look back and find that her journey has been entirely different from anyone else's, for each artist takes a path into herself to a uniquely private destination.

It is only human nature, however, to want quick results, to try to find a shortcut through the whole tedious process of producing excellent writing. Why can't I be as great as Tolstoy *now?* Well, a voice whispers from within, maybe I *am.* Maybe this very sentence I am in the act of composing will someday be memorized by schoolchildren and —

Suddenly the act of creation comes to a halt. What happened? The contact with the deeper stratum of myself that the act of art requires has just been rudely broken by the shrill transmission of that ham operator, my ego. As we saw in Chapter 4, when the ego abandons true partnership and attempts to wrest control from the unconscious, the block springs up, impenetrable. That mischievous child has stuck its foot firmly in front of my "vaulting ambition, which o'erleaps itself," and I have fallen flat on my face.

Self-consciousness of any kind, but especially of the prematurely self-congratulatory sort, is death to spontaneous performance, whether the activity is pole vaulting or writing a poem. Katherine Mansfield, who took the ethics of artistic creation very seriously, once noted:

> I wonder why it should be so difficult to be humble. I do not think I am a good writer; I realize my faults better than anyone else could realize them. . . . And yet, when I have finished a story and before I have begun another, I catch myself *preening* my feathers. It is disheartening. There seems to be some bad old pride in my heart; a root of it that puts out a thick shoot on the slightest provocation. . . . This interferes very much with work. One can't be calm, clear, good as one must be, while it goes on. . . . It's a kind of excitement within one, which shouldn't be there. . . . And anything that I write in this mood will be no good; it will be full of *sediment.*

Though there is a clear difference in degree between the mood Mansfield is describing and the excesses quoted at the beginning of this chapter, it is still the same creature: the state of inflation, just as pernicious to the artist as that of self-loathing.

But isn't it natural to feel pleasure from accomplishment, and beyond that, satisfaction, even love of one's work and the desire to be recognized for what one has done? Isn't this the true antidote to the self-hate that throttles so much creativity? What can be wrong with the urge to excel, to want to aim high and be the best one can be, to want to have one's work read and appreciated by the widest possible audience?

Undeniably, ambition and belief in one's future prospects play a vital, positive role in any writing life. Without the deep inner conviction of talent and worth, no writer has the strength to endure the endless rejections, insults, bad reviews, and corkscrew twists and turns of a profession in which, more than any other, advancement depends almost entirely on the judgment (often the whim) of others — editors, critics, readers. And it is not just a matter of having a favorable opinion of one's own talents. I question whether there has ever been a writer or any other artist who hasn't cherished the secret conviction that he or she is the absolute greatest.

Take, for example, the sculptor Benjamin Haydon, friend of John Keats, as described by Keats's biographer Aileen Ward: "What [Haydon] described in his journals as 'irresistible, perpetual, continued urgings of future greatness' used to shoot through him with such intensity that he could only 'lift up his heart and thank God' for these assurances of divine favour." Another Romantic example is our old friend Coleridge, as described by his friend Sir Humphry Davy:

> His will is probably less than ever commensurate with his ability. Brilliant images of greatness float upon his mind . . . agitated by every breeze, and modified by every sunbeam. He talked, in the course of one hour, of beginning three works, and he recited the poem of *Christabel,* unfinished, as I had before heard it.

Coleridge's *Biographia Literaria* makes instructive reading not only as a potpourri of shrewd literary judgments but as self-exposure on the grand scale, a classic combination of intense vulnerability and panic-stricken self-aggrandizement of the sort often found in the writer paralyzed by excessive ambition.

But for every Haydon who unabashedly advertises his own consummate virtues, thousands of more circumspect writers whisper the same sweet words in the privacy of their souls. Overambition in this sense might be considered simply a problem of personal management; a writer is judged modest to the degree that she or he is able to hide the true state of affairs inside. And if all do it, then where's the harm?

The key, as in so many other areas of creative endeavor, lies in moderation — and especially in not daydreaming on the job. Writer's block occurs as a healthy check only on an intrusive and persistent ambition that exceeds your present abilities by too great an order of magnitude. You stare hypnotized at the page as the voice within composes not the story you are writing but the rave reviews it will receive in the country's greatest literary journal. Such grandiosity will kill you at the start, or any other time.

The way out of this dead-end alley is to forget yourself and surrender your intrusive ego to the work at hand. You must junk the Nobel Prize speech, return your eyes to the paper, and begin the mundane task of composing words. "One *must* avoid ambition *in order to* write," Cynthia Ozick has said. "Otherwise something else is the goal: some kind of power beyond the power of language. And the power of language, it seems to me, is the only kind of power a writer is entitled to."

Grandiosity typically attaches itself to single projects removed from the rest of the oeuvre. Every writer has The Book, usually unfinished, never so much a real project as a barge loaded down with a cargo of inflated, immature ambition. Some of these books do get completed, and many are published — usually those of already established authors who are writing backward from the favorable reviews of their previous books. Conceived in a state of inflation, these curiously still-born works (full of the "sediment" Mansfield mentions) leave the reader who thinks for himself uneasy and dissatisfied. They are forced, lifeless, and profoundly unrealized. If you have a project that was written out of the empty well of ambition, there may not be any way to reapproach it in a modest, focused, refining spirit. Inflated works, often moribund, are better discarded.

What if the outrageous visions of future greatness persist? And what — here comes the seductive voice again — if they are prescient, wholly justified? What if they should come true in the end? James Joyce declared early on, through his mouthpiece Stephen Dedalus, that he was going to "forge in the smithy of my soul the uncreated conscience of my race" — a highly impressive statement of intent. With the writing of *Ulysses*, that grandiose announcement was apparently fulfilled. It took Joyce ten years to write this book and the rest of his life (another seventeen years) to complete *Finnegans Wake* (which some heretics consider an inflated work), but write them he did. Wasn't he then justified in having these dreams of future accomplishment and even in boldly proclaiming them to the world? Haven't many great artists, such as Wagner and Picasso, been monsters of egocentricity? What, in fact, is the difference between healthy ambition and destructive grandiosity?

The answer can best be found in an investigation of the gray area lying between a balanced individual's confidence in himself, his hopes and dreams, and the personality disorder of extreme egotism or narcissism, a dis-ease of the soul not to be mistaken with mere selfishness or self-absorption (both fairly common traits in artists of all sorts). Narcissism, in the nonspecialist's meaning I give it here (what one writer has aptly dubbed "ego-ridden powerlessness"), is a malady to which we all occasionally succumb, but only in a few does it persist past all cure.

THE FALSE MUSE NARCISSUS

The ego is the caricature people mistake for the self, the ego is
the fraud, the actor, the transvestite of the self.

— ANAÏS NIN

Blocks are simply forms of egotism.

— LAWRENCE DURRELL

He had a very high opinion of himself. Sometimes it made him
look like a pygmy.

— STANISLAW JERZY LEC

It may seem a paradox that paralyzing ambition is a function
of an unnaturally inflated ego. If self-hatred destroys creativity,
wouldn't an egotistical person necessarily have a higher opinion of himself than ordinary mortals? Wouldn't he be in ample
possession of the self-acceptance and self-confidence so critical to the act of art?

The answer is no. The truth is that a "big ego" conceals a
deep and overriding sense of worthlessness, just as the seemingly hang-loose habit of "procrastination" hides a rule-bound
compulsive personality. The egotism has formed as a compensation, a kind of daily self-armoring against an unbearable
inner feeling of self-loathing. Egotism is a mask of superiority
designed to hide — as much from its owner, significantly, as
from others — the true face, inferiority. Lacking a center, the
egotistical personality swings wildly between the twin psychic
poles of grandiosity and utter self-contempt.

In this context, worship of the self is a kind of pathetic
psychic cargo cult that fools no one, least of all the worshiper
himself. The nature of any psychological compensation is that
it can never genuinely *satisfy;* it is only a substitute, in this case
for genuine self-respect. Soon the inferiority begins to reassert
its dominance. And the more insistent the feelings of worthlessness, the more frantic become the ego's attempts to repress
them. The energy the organism must expend in continuing
this cover-up is excessive and debilitating. It leaves little time

for any other meaningful activity, least of all creative work, which rises from a bedrock of self-confidence.

Here again writer's block has the potential, usually not properly heeded, of working positive, healing effects on a psyche headed for narcissistic entropy. By halting the act of art, the block asserts that the emperor has no clothes. By stripping off false vanity, it provides the suffering writer a clue that she should be examining herself at a deeper level than that of pipe dreams. But such an examination is just what the narcissistic personality knows it must avoid at all costs, because it means touching the psychic equivalent of an open wound. Probing the deeper level means that the inadmissible secret sense of inferiority would have to be faced. So most often the writer's attention is quickly displaced from the seesawing self-esteem to the block itself, which is then blamed for all subsequent problems. Meanwhile, the less work accomplished, the larger the fantasies become. The projected opus will not merely be good, it will be the greatest accomplishment of the century, of all recorded time. And so on.

But all fantasies require some fuel to keep them aloft. And when none is forthcoming in reality, artificial measures must be taken to sustain the false system. The classic shortcut between excessive ambition and unrealized accomplishment is the abuse of alcohol or drugs, which keeps the ego euphoric and unnaturally inflated.

NARCISSISM AND ALCOHOL: THE MISSING LINK

> This cunning disease offers feelings of instant success and riotous fame to one who lusts after them.
> — DONALD NEWLOVE

> Drunkenness is a substitute for art; it is in itself a low form of creation.
> — CYRIL CONNOLLY

We all enjoy mood enhancers (or depressants) because they make us feel good in a special way: they erase our usual inhibitions and open the door to the unconscious. But there is always the danger that one will gradually become fixed on the means, not the end, feeling unable to contact the unconscious in any other way. Then brief euphoria leads ever deeper into immense despair. (One of the most moving descriptions of this psychological Gordian knot can be found in Charles Jackson's forgotten classic, *The Lost Weekend*.) For every would-be writer who is an alcoholic or a drug user, there is someone who was once a writer but is now an alcoholic or an addict. Dependence on a substance is a full-time occupation, and no one writes well while chronically drunk or stoned.

Though there are many theories — psychological, biochemical, even genetic — about the root causes of alcoholism and addiction, a childish egotism that stubbornly refuses to mature with physical aging is often a symptom of this mysterious disorder. After all, what other medium than alcohol or drugs best preserves and magnifies the characteristic adolescent mood swings between elation and despair?

In *Those Drinking Days*, an unsparing and perceptive account of a drinking-writing symbiosis, Donald Newlove states that he justified his habits by the fact that "all the American writers and poets I admired drank as I did. . . . I took all their manias and ulcers as badges of glory." The romantic linkage of art with alcohol was severed for him only after years of painful rehabilitation: "That the greatest writing is made out of loneliness and despair magnified by booze is an idea for arrested adolescents." The reader who requires further evidence is directed to Tom Dardis's *The Thirsty Muse*, a detailed documentation of the way in which progressive alcoholism destroyed the art of four major writers.

But is there any truth at all to the popular notion that an essential connection exists between genius and self-destruction? Let us examine this tenet more closely, for it can exert a lethal influence on an impressionable and sensitive person who happens also to be a writer.

THE MYTH OF THE SUFFERING GENIUS

We all grew up with romance in our heads
The Romance that the secret of success
Was genius, blazing gifts lighting the world.
Genius, the noble individual
Long-haired, peculiar and long suffering,
A kind of Christ, in fact, or Fisher-King . . .
— DELMORE SCHWARTZ

How [can] a genius be happy, normal — above all, long-lived?
— CHARLES JACKSON, *The Lost Weekend*

The aura of "genius" that hangs over literary endeavors like a poison cloud is intimately related to the problem of egotism. What is a genius? A genius, goes the common thinking, is somebody whose special gifts place him or her above the rest of the world and its petty cares. Therefore, special treatment must be accorded the genius because of these gifts and the sensitivity that, it is assumed, tortures him or her daily. (This reasoning is also a handy club for keeping spouses and lovers of the Sensitive One in line.)

A concomitant line of thought — and here is the link to alcoholism — is that geniuses, besides being sensitive and having special gifts, are tormented, self-destructive souls who take to drink, drugs, and ultimately suicide to find relief from the existential angst of being artists. This is Rilke's "demons and angels" fallacy, that the suffering of artists is intrinsic and occurs on a higher level than it does for "ordinary" people. In any other profession, it would seem self-evident that alcoholism or madness would be a minus, not a plus, but the arts have been infected by a curious romanticism that is perpetuated by canny (or at best, self-deceiving) artists along with their often surprisingly gullible biographers.

Amazingly, the notion is still prevalent that alcoholism, for example, and the deep depression that can follow sudden alcohol withdrawal testify to the "terrible truth that the greatest art is often produced by the most tormented of souls," to quote one starry-eyed newspaper account of a writer's drying-out experience. For my money, no one has punctured this last bubble of artistic inflation more effectively than Donald Newlove: "You might as well say about a Bronx housewife on the sauce that the warmth she longs for has been exiled to the outer edges of life in the America of her time, it's that empty an alibi."

What is the source of these gross misapprehensions about the way art is made and the people who make it? A century and a half ago, Charles Lamb speculated in his essay "Sanity of True Genius":

> The ground of the mistake is, that men, finding in the raptures of the higher poetry a condition of exaltation to which they have no parallel in their own experience, besides the spurious resemblance of it in dreams and fevers, impute a state of dreaminess and fever to the poet. But the true poet dreams being awake. He is not possessed by his subject, but has dominion over it.

The logical extension of Lamb's thesis is Gustave Flaubert's self-command, never equaled for its succinctness and good sense: "Be regular and orderly in your life like a bourgeois, so that you may be violent and original in your work."

This kind of homely wisdom does not fit conveniently with the sentimental image of the artist's tragic lot, to which chronic writer's block makes such a perfect accessory. A writer who can't write — what, after all, could be more tragic than that? Now, it can be safely said that life, for everyone, contains a strong tragic vein, but the true suffering of the artist lies in enduring the daily anxiety and tedium of "turning sentences around," of living through the unbearably slow development of his or her abilities.

There are many sensitive people who suffer terribly, but not all or most or even half of them are artists. Those artists who, as humans, are saddled with the afflictions of mental illness or alcoholism create their work in spite of their infirmities, not because of them. That prosaic struggle, not the falsely romantic patina of their disabilities, holds the true potential for heroism. Franz Kafka created great works of art in spite of his conspicuous self-hatred, not because of it. By making his inner struggles the raw material of his art, he achieved a great victory over them.

Still, it could be argued, what about poet A and writer Y, or dozens upon dozens of others? How do we account for the sheer number of writers who have succumbed to alcoholism, madness, or suicide? Strictly by proportion the count is rather high compared to other professions. Doesn't that prove there is a connection between art and self-destruction? The subject is too complex for full consideration here, but a correlation does seem to exist between a sheltered, intense childhood environment and a propensity for artistic expression, with self-absorption and childlike behavior persisting well into adulthood. Some artists, in fact, seem to enjoy long — that is, lifelong — childhoods, a quality that promotes the close and ongoing relationship with the unconscious.

There is, however, a distinction between child*like* and child*ish*. Submitting one's talent to a long, exacting training, maintaining and carrying it through to fulfillment, is an adult undertaking requiring an inner orientation very different than the childish egotism arising from feelings of inferiority. Narcissism is a problem of personality that must be dealt with on human terms, not rationalized as the badge of genius. To paraphrase John Stuart Mill, we are men and women first, artists second. To mature as a writer requires maturing first as a person. The mark of a civilized person is not education or accomplishments but how well one has faced and civilized one's own nature. Artists can be sensitive and perceptive about other people to beat all, but in this other life task they start at zero just like everybody else.

True works of art, finally, do not spring from a desire to be famous; they grow out of a deeper stratum of emotional and spiritual resources within the human being. Keats, struggling with his long-delayed, chronically blocked *Hyperion*, was urged by his friend the previously mentioned narcissist Haydon to finish the poem regardless. In reply, Keats

> announced to Haydon . . . that he had resolved "never to write for the sake of writing, or making a poem." . . . The more Keats struggled with his poem, the more he realized that great poetry could not be written out of mere great ambition or even some gift of noble language, but only out of a knowledge of life which he had not yet achieved.

Keats's block represented the deeper knowledge of his unconscious that his abilities and experience were not yet on a par with his high intentions for the poem. Countless other writers have had to set aside their Towering Achievements of former years and fix their eyes resolutely on more immediately accessible channels for their talent. The opposite of inflation is small, steady steps during which ego is subordinated to work. For the overambitious, less will always be better than more. Aiming lower makes the target easier to hit.

Consider the example of Wordsworth, whose projected magnum opus, *The Recluse*, was to be the vehicle of his own self-designated role as poet-prophet of *his* age. Now the ego may cherish such a goal (preferably in private) as much as it pleases, but it will not be allowed to inject "greatness" into any work — and was not, in Wordsworth's case. Understandably unable to make his naked ambition materialize as art, he produced something else instead, the preliminary announcement of the great work, the bit that didn't count, which turned out not half bad. We dream our *Recluses*. Then we write our *Preludes*.

7

The Myth of
Unlimited Possibilities

——— ❖ ———

A young Adonis, golden haired
Stands dreaming on the verge of strife
Magnificently unprepared
For the long littleness of life.
— FRANCES CORNFORD

MANY WRITERS and would-be writers experience chronic block not simply out of grandiose expectations but also from an overwhelming vagueness about what they are actually *able* to do, as opposed to what they might someday do, if they get around to it. Naturally enough, the best way to maintain this comforting ignorance of one's true creative limits is by doing nothing and imagining everything. Actually to put words to paper is to abandon the divine world of the possible and enter the profane world of the real, with all its trivial limitations. To take action, to write, means turning one's back on the never-never land of adolescence, where anything and everything is always about to happen, could happen, but usually never quite does happen.

The poet and essayist Wendell Berry has identified not one but two creative muses: the Muse of Inspiration and the Muse of Realization. This chapter will explore the psychological set of those "potential" writers who never quite get from the temple of Muse Number 1 to that of Muse Number 2, a condition that might be called the daydreaming block.

Daydreaming and fantasizing are essential to the creative process. They make up the precreative experience, the incubation period that precedes the act of art. But images in the mind are nothing in themselves; they must be made manifest to be considered art. A person who prolongs fantasizing indefinitely floats in a diffuse and generalized dreaminess that never finds a focus or expression in art.

The number of potential writers who never succeed in breaking out of this comfortable nest of dreams is legion. Typically, the person is a talented beginner who writes scraps and fragments of stories, poems, or screenplays but is unable to develop or finish his ideas. The work in progress is often a vehicle for fantasies of grandeur associated with its future reception by the world. Since to complete the project would make it only too clear whether one had really produced the Great Work, the would-be writer's only recourse in protecting his narcissism is to leave everything he starts unfinished so that he can sustain his fantasies. Here the playful child has been co-opted into the lesser service of immature vanity. If the divine child refuses to become a profane adult, if the unconscious is kept constantly busy churning out puerile daydreams of glory, there is nothing left over to produce a sustained work of imagination.

A related phenomenon occurs in the university setting when graduate students, after a prolonged course of study, find themselves strangely unable to write their dissertations. The field must be revisited, more books must be read, related avenues of inquiry must be pursued. There are various reasons for this common malaise, not the least of which are making the transition from taking notes to actual writing (a problem I will take up in the next chapter) and having to run the marathon without benefit of a warm-up. But a deeper issue frequently emerges as well. This is the unavoidable fact that no initiation rite in life is more shockingly abrupt than giving up the casual delights of student life and entering the structured adult world of duties, restrictions on personal freedom, and career pressures and compromises. Understandably, people balk at the prospect of this drastic and unappealing change of habits. Thus we have "thesis block," a time-honored (though by definition completely unconscious) means of prolonging a carefree extended childhood as well as exacerbating long-buried feelings of inadequacy and ambivalence in accepting judgment from authority figures and passing over the shadow line into becoming such an authority figure oneself.

The reluctance to abandon the magic world of imagined future prospects for the gray world of real acts constitutes a kind of existential stage fright at the threshold of life. One is never quite ready to make an entrance because that means one would have to commit oneself to playing a single role and no other. One lives one's possibilities in the imagination because one is afraid to test them in the outside world. Milan Kundera said of one of his characters: "The more he suffers from the fear of trying for something modest and well defined, the more he wants to conquer the world, the infinity of the undefined, the indefinedness of the infinite." Over a lifetime, this almost universally experienced phenomenon of adolescence can harden into a permanent posture as the Hamletesque split between *posse* and *esse* widens into a chasm. And overweening ambition is a frequent companion to this state of mind.

The inability to give up the world of the possible for the world of the actual has been labeled the *puer aeternus*, or "eternal youth," syndrome by the Jungian analyst Marie Louise von Franz. According to von Franz, the typical *puer aeternus* (or *puella aeterna;* plenty of women manifest the same symptoms) embodies

a form of neurosis which H. G. Baynes has described as the "provisional life," that is, the strange attitude and feeling that one is *not yet* in real life. For the time being one is doing this or that, but whether it is a woman or a job, it is *not yet* what is really wanted, and there is always the fantasy that sometime in the future the real thing will come about. If this attitude is prolonged, it means a constant inner refusal to commit oneself to the moment. . . . The one thing dreaded throughout by such a type of man is to be bound to anything whatever. There is a terrific fear of being pinned down, of entering space and time completely, and of being the one human being that one is.

The extreme examples of the eternal youth type are familiar enough and even possess a certain severe beauty of form: the golden hippie hardened into middle-aged street person; the fifty-year-old surfer with skin like a crocodile's; the coffee-house novelist with pages 1 and 2 of his notebook filled and the rest forever empty. But there is also a generous portion of Peter Pan in every person who does not immediately take up job, marriage, and family in his or her early adult years, and this group includes large numbers of artists and would-be artists. Other people grow up entirely on the outside while their inside remains childlike and untouched, swirling with Walter Mitty fantasies. Among this group are the conscientious toilers in other professions who rope off a secret corner of their souls in which to swoop and soar in fantasies of creating art, if only they had the time.

After perfectionism and narcissism (and feeding into both), the eternal youth phenomenon is one of the cornerstones of writer's block. By not writing, one is obeying the urgent inner command not to define oneself, not to grow and develop into that sad and limited creature, a minor (or possibly even a never-published) poet or whatever. Instead, one stays interestingly, *potentially* great the rest of one's life. It is a phenomenon that occurs not merely among people who daydream a great deal and write very little but also (as I will discuss later) among people who show tremendous early promise and have lavish attention focused on their first works. To leave the bright limelight of precocity and enter the drab world of slow maturation can be a frightening, impossible step to take. Fitzgerald's dictum, "There are no second acts in American lives," applies ecumenically here. For a *puer aeternus,* Act One is the whole show, curtain calls included.

Most commonly, eternal youths of every age and description produce no works at all, preferring instead to nourish a sense of their own specialness. The hero of Robert Musil's *Man Without Qualities,* a classic *puer,* "feels himself to be like a stride that could be taken in any direction." To such a person, "concreteness suggests craftsmanship, and getting down to craftsmanship means dirtying one's hands."

To be fair, most serious artists in their early years partake of some of these qualities. Many evolving writers experience a prolonged and dreamy development in which work comes in painful fits and starts. But even though the temptation to slide backward into undemanding fantasy is strong, these awkward beginners are gradually developing, though with unbelievable slowness; at the end of the century, the cereus blossom will open — but not a minute before. In this way the time of fantasy and inactivity often proves to be the extended incubation period that is eventually, in one's thirties and forties or even later, superseded by a productive career. Still other artists manage to grow up, after a fashion, within their work while remaining eternal youths in other areas of their lives; in later years, alcoholism or mental illness may undermine their abilities or cut short their working (and actual) lives.

How, then, is the "real writer" different from the writer-to-be who carries his fragments of stories to the café like talismanic objects every day for years and years? They are hardly different at all, except that, in the case of the writer, *finally* something happens: a corner is turned, paradise is lost, and the eternal child enters the world of age and death. But the breakthrough does not usually occur until other emotional bonds are broken as well; for here the very ability to carry through the act of art is absolutely linked to personal maturation.

Let us take the familiar case of the Brontë sisters and their brother Branwell as an example. Charlotte, Emily, Anne, and Branwell enjoyed the archetypal writer's childhood in their widower father's parsonage, a sheltered, exaggeratedly insular environment in which, for lack of outside visitors or amusement, they invented the land of Angria, an imaginary African kingdom with an elaborate history and a vast array of characters. Led always in their fantasies by Branwell, chief instigator and the most conspicuously brilliant of the lot, the Brontë children recorded their Angrian chronicles in volume upon volume of minuscule coded script.

When childhood ended, the sisters proceeded in turn to their humble jobs as governesses, while Branwell, the young star, awaited his shining destiny as a famous author. It never came. He took and lost many menial positions, became an alcoholic, and died early with none of his ambitions realized. A prolific and talented writer as a child, he was hopelessly blocked as a man. His sisters, perhaps because they were women and thus automatically excluded from the heavy burden of worldly expectations Branwell's father had placed on his shoulders, were able, by dint of slow and painful labor, to convert the images of their childhood Nirvana into adult art, thereby winning their own victories against a seductive and claustrophobic past. Branwell was unable to perform this rite of passage. In an unfinished fragment of a novel, he gave his hero this familiar *puer*'s lament: "There are plenty of paths in this life. Which shall I take? Only they all require walking to get on them." After what he called, in this same fragment, the "summit of childhood," Branwell could not bear to descend (as he saw it) from the world of infinite possibility into the world of limited acts.

Those eternal youths who, unlike Branwell, live on, bear the weight of their aborted emotional development and unrealized talent. As Samuel Coleridge's own *puer* son Hartley put it in a mournful sonnet:

> Nor child, nor man,
> Nor youth, nor sage, I find my head is grey,
> For I have lost the race I never ran:
> A rathe December blights my lagging May;

> And still I am a child, tho' I be old,
> Time is my debtor for my years untold.

Viewed from this perspective, the life of an eternal youth is a sad one, but that looking-back judgment fails to acknowledge the fact that the inner experience itself is inexpressibly seductive. Try telling Peter Pan to give up flying and walk from point A to point B, and he will laugh. And yet that pedestrian act is exactly what he must do.

COMING DOWN TO EARTH

Typically, full-fledged *pueri* (as distinct from those who dream of writing while holding other employment) are not busy people. They have too much, not too little, time in which to write. There is a trust fund, an easy part-time job (this includes teaching), or some other source of minimal financial support in the background — the perfect arrangement for a writer, no? Not necessarily. Those who have the most free time to devote to writing are often precisely the ones who are least able to exploit this opportunity; the lack of boundaries in their lives causes them to flounder. For the unformed person, limitless time offers just more rope to hang himself with.

Baby's first step, for the eternal youth, often means simply committing herself to work of any sort, even if it is not writing. The experience of submitting to the rigors of a real job, no matter how menial, can have a beneficial carryover to writing. When free time is suddenly confined to an early hour each day or on the weekend, it gains a value all the unending empty months never had. If you are such a person and have been able to accomplish next to nothing with all the free time in the world, the constraints imposed by a job may allow you to accomplish far more in those few precious hours that are left. You are entering the world of *limits*, which paradoxically liberates you from the prison of limitlessness. Within this structure, which most of us need badly in our lives, you can allow yourself an hour a day — before work, during lunch hour, on the weekend — to "play."

Suppose, however, you are experiencing the chief *puer* symptom — chronic daydreaming about writing or being a writer, but very little writing — without partaking of the rest of the syndrome. Suppose you live the "provisional" life only in terms of writing and nothing else. What is the day-to-day manifestation of this block likely to be?

If you are experiencing many fantasies about writing without producing anything, you are also likely to be afflicted with the chronic psychological sets already described — namely, the master-slave dispute coupled with wildly inflated expectations. After a period of immersion in fantasies about writing (and, naturally, about yourself as a world-famous writer), you may suffer a severe attack of guilt when the plain reality of no writing produced asserts itself. You lash yourself as a lazy, worthless creature and resolve on the spot to get up at dawn and write three, five, eight hours a day for the rest of your natural life. This habit is by no means confined to novice writers. When Coleridge decided that he ought to impose a "manly consistency" on his numerous unfulfilled plans and dreams, what project did he order himself to do? Two volumes of Latin verse imitations, which fortunately did not get written.

To be grounded is not the same as sentencing yourself to the salt mines — though eternal youths typically confuse the two. Even if you get as far as rising at dawn, of course, you will certainly not be able to carry out the rest of the drastic regimen; the block immediately rises at this futile attempt at self-tyranny. Instead of understanding it as a signal to modify your self-demands to something closer to your real-life personal habits, you mistake this healthy and practical reaction for more laziness. After a long and fruitless struggle against the block (which in this context is the only real sign so far of your creativity), you slide slowly back into the comfortable, seductive ooze of your daydreams.

This cycle can easily go on for years, if not a lifetime. How to break it? First of all, if it is a habit of some duration, you must face the difficult fact that it will not transform itself overnight. The transition from making dreams to making things is a developmental process that occurs gradually, much like physical growth, over a period of years. Neither can be speeded up artificially. If you attempt to pole-vault over your natural rate of development with imaginings of not-yet-achieved grandeur, you can expect the process to take that much longer. And since fantasy is the root of the act of art, it is not a habit to be broken but to be gone into more deeply, rechanneled to the demands of one's work. Fantasy is the raw material of art as well as of daydreams. Producing a work of art, however, means getting your hands dirty.

Arriving at the childlike joy of creative expression, then, sometimes requires traveling in the opposite direction — to maturation, as a person and as an artist. Experiencing completion by working or assuming other mundane responsibilities can bring you either to writing (if that is what your deepest self wants) or to some other activity that finally involves you in life. For the writer, involvement in life always means putting a word on a piece of paper to initiate the act of art, and then putting enough words down after that first one to produce a finished work — short, long, or medium-sized. Length is unimportant; completion is.

When you first take up your burden of limits, it will often appear that you are not going anywhere. In fact, the developmental process is proceeding at a steady rate. Your only requirement is to keep writing — no matter if it seems to you that you are the slowest writer in the world, even if your rate is only one story a year. If you can write and finish just one thing, you have taken a step away from your ghostly dreamland. And each piece you complete, no matter how pitiful it seems compared to the great opus you can *imagine* (and possibly even write the first paragraph of), takes you that many more steps along in your gradual conversion from dreamer into writer. An eternal youth, after all, is an enchanted creature, half in the other world and half in this one; to reverse your bewitchment, you must perform some spells of your own. And writing is exactly that: a hex against oblivion.

Here is one such spell, for those afflicted. Choose any one

of the dozens of story, play, or poem fragments in your personal collection and explore the possibility of finishing it. Be careful not to force an ending or simply stop. Put your heart into a genuine finish and allow yourself the experience of closure, an important rite of passage for a *puer*. Once completed, your work loses the *potential* of greatness and gains the *actuality* of being what it is, and nothing else. If you can finish one, try finishing others. Remember that if you suffer from this type of block, it is more valuable (because it is harder) to finish one work than to begin a dozen others. You may discover that the act of completing your work has become a habit, a grounded activity.

If you can endure the sentence of enchantment without giving up, you stand an excellent chance of becoming a real human being — not as beautiful as a swan but far more powerful. This metamorphosis will happen only if you first submit yourself to those two mundane humiliations: beginning your writing, however fearful that seems, and carrying it through to completion, no matter how long it takes you. Out of that tiresome, unglamorous struggle comes grace.

8

Notes and Plans That Refuse to Make a Book

———— ❖ ————

"And all your notes," said Dorothea . . . "All those rows of volumes — will you not make up your mind what part of them you will use, and begin to write the book which will make your vast knowledge useful to the world?"
— GEORGE ELIOT, *Middlemarch*

F OR MANY WRITERS the act of taking notes — or even that enjoyable indulgence in freeform reading known by the dignified title "research" — is more than a prelude to the main event. Mysteriously, it comes to supersede the act of writing and becomes the hurdle they are never able to clear.

Rightly or wrongly, we tend to view the chronic notetaker as a certain kind of personality — a less than attractive kind. Eliot's Mr. Casaubon, addressed by his wife in the opening quotation, embodies our notions of the archetypal notetaker — fussy, rigid, and anal retentive. A real-life example was the ethnologist John Peabody Harrington (immortalized in his ex-wife Carobeth Laird's memoirs, *Encounter with an Angry God*), who filled warehouse after warehouse at the Smithsonian with tons of dusty notes on Native American languages but was rarely able, for unexplained reasons, to "write them up."

A less extreme form of the notetaking disease flourishes in writers of every kind — poets and novelists as well as scholars and journalists. The notes in question can represent voluminous research for a historical novel, cryptic phrases and words that don't quite add up to anything but sound awfully promising, jottings on characters, fictitious family trees and labyrinthine plot flowcharts. And we must not leave out the famous shoebox full of index cards, common accessory of "thesis block," that the hapless graduate student is cursed to cart around until she fulfills the terms of her enchantment. What miracle (or what desperate pact with the Devil) will transform the smeared, dog-eared, coffee-stained ink scratches into a coherent work made up of complete sentences marching proudly from beginning straight through to triumphant conclusion?

The only magic that can bring about this transformation is the act of composition, a process so removed from notetaking that the two might not be considered part of the same experience. This is the real point. Notetaking is not the same thing as writing. Taking notes is a mechanical-analytical act, not a creative one, even when the notes do not detail hard data but the soarings of your imagination. Because of the qualitative difference between these two acts, it's trickier than you might think to make the transition from one to the other. In fact, it's sometimes far easier to jump straight from writing one piece to writing another on an entirely different subject than to proceed from notes on a story to the story itself. The act of writing engenders more writing, and taking notes is by no means a warm-up for this act. The tortured graduate student might be better off warming up for her thesis by writing a short article on a related topic than by indulging in yet another Talmudic perusal of her notes.

There is a further problem. Old notes, like old hamburger, congeal. Over time, notes lose their tenuous connection to the dynamic creation of a work and settle into their own rigid reality. The writer, in turn, no longer connected to the inner wellspring of thoughts and associations that informed the notes, begins to relate solely to the notes themselves, which have grown strangely colorless, like seashells taken out of the water. Natalia Ginzburg has spoken to this problem:

> I kept a notebook in which I wrote down some of the details I had discovered, or little similes, or episodes which I promised myself I would use in stories. I would write in my notebook . . . "His curls like bunches of grapes," "Red and black blankets on an unmade bed," "A pale face like a peeled potato." But I discovered how difficult it was to use these phrases when I was writing a story. The notebook became a kind of museum of phrases that were crystallized and embalmed and very difficult to use. I tried endlessly to slip the red and black blankets or the curls like bunches of grapes into a story but I never managed to. So the notebook was no help to me. I realised that in this vocation there is no such thing as "savings." . . . When someone writes a story he should throw the best of everything into it, the best of whatever he possessed and has seen, all the best things that he has accumulated throughout his life. If you carry details around inside yourself for a long time without making use of them, they wear out and waste away. Not only details but everything, all your clever ideas and notions.

Why, then, do we experience the desire to cling to our notes instead of simply getting on with the writing? First, because we have already developed a certain notetaking momentum, and it is easier to stay in this mode than to switch to a radically different one. Second, because those notes possess one unassailable advantage: they are there, on paper, in black and white. For the writer who fears that lonely first encounter with a blank page, the temptation to hang on to what has already been captured in the net of awareness — the notes — is irresistible. They become a security blanket, protection against the horrors of the unknown and the spontaneous, which the writer must face during actual composition. Notes allow the writer to stay in control — though accomplishing nothing — by grimly continuing to practice kicks while clutching the edge of the swimming pool.

Chronic notetaking that never develops into finished work is not necessarily the same as the aversion to completion that characterizes the eternal youth sensibility. Rather, it is habitual among people who are obsessive and controlling, who are deathly afraid of losing that control, of opening themselves up to the experience of discovering the unexpected inside themselves. "What people . . . do out of fear of irrational elements in themselves as well as in other people is *to put tools and mechanics between themselves and the unconscious world,*" the psychiatrist Rollo May observed. "This protects them from being grasped by the frightening and threatening aspects of the irrational experience." The anxiety that even the prospect of such an encounter generates is enough to send such a person scurrying back to the notebook for yet a further round of fragmented, unconnected (but controllable) bits of shorthand about what he is planning, someday, to write.

Obviously, there is notetaking and notetaking. The foregoing examples represent the extreme end of the spectrum and not the middle, where a nice set of notes is a solid launching pad from which to begin the composition of a new work. You do not need to reproach yourself for such a habit; it is necessary and useful. Here we are concerned with the obsessive notetaking that, by its very difference from the creative process, tends to possess the writer and become an end in itself. The challenge to the chronic notetaker is to overcome his fears. Can he be persuaded to let go the edge of the swimming pool and kick off, unsupported, into deep water?

The preliminary stages that lead up to the act of composition generally fall in this order: (1) The germ of an attractive idea surfaces irresistibly in the writer's consciousness. (2) An indeterminate period of gestation takes place in which various details and elaborations suggest themselves that he may or may not be noting down. (3) He begins to write.

The chronic notetaker is likely to bog down in stage 2, unwittingly locking his potential butterfly inside a stone cocoon that often takes the form of an outline, a book proposal, or a fellowship application. That is why hundreds of thousands more proposals have been written in this world than actual books. The Irish writer Frank O'Connor made it a point never to record more than four lines of notes before beginning a story, because "if you make the subject of a story twelve or fourteen lines, that's a treatment. You've already committed yourself to the sort of character, the sort of surroundings, and the moment you've committed yourself, the story is already written. It has ceased to be fluid, you can't design it any longer, you can't model it." Anthony Burgess uses basically the same strategy for beginning a novel: "I chart a little first — lists of names, rough synopses of chapters, and so on. But one daren't overplan; so many things are generated by the sheer act of writing."

Once committed to paper, an outline or other analytical matrix can kill a half-born work by systematizing it too early in the gestation process. There's nothing left to imagine; the joy of surprise and discovery that is such a striking feature of the act of art has been co-opted before it even has a chance to begin.

Sometimes the block that prevents you from making the transition from notes to writing is there because the project you have contemplated is too overwhelming and ambitious for your present level of ability. This is what happened to Coleridge, who was forever accepting advances from publishers for outlines of twelve-volume metaphysical or geographical works that never quite materialized. The more grandiose the plan, the more comprehensive the table of contents, the more immense the block.

Even in imaginative writing organization and planning are helpful and necessary, especially in blocking out a long work such as a novel — but how easily and insidiously these means become ends in themselves! After staring at the empty page, you turn back with pleasure and relief to the busywork of fussing with those potsherds, your notes. Taking notes becomes the perfect sanctuary in which to hide so that you can avoid facing the fact that your ego is overdetermining what you are planning to write. An outline or set of notes that paralyzes you instead of inspiring you can be read as your conscious attempt to exert total control over the situation instead of letting go, surrendering to its possibilities and allowing yourself to be guided (usually in a different direction than the notes might indicate) by your creative energies.

Suppose you have written an outline for a novel that calls for a certain amount of factual or historical research. You go to the library, read extensively, take copious notes. It's fun, it's structured, and it's safe. But it is not synonymous with the creative act. Unfortunately, the security of notetaking is so addictive that the more you do, the harder it gets to go back to the scary part — writing. One way to avoid this impasse is not to give up regular creative activity while you are in the midst of taking notes. Allot a portion of your time every day to writing something else, and the transition from planning to actual composing in your major project will be a hundred times easier.

Or suppose you interrupted a writing career to work or raise children. For years you have carried the idea for an ambitious project, but all you have been able to do is make notes on it. When the time finally arrives to begin, you may find it virtually impossible to write because all those years you have been honing your skills in an entirely different activity — taking notes. In effect, you were training for the Boston marathon by describing the act of running instead of doing a little running every day. A better way to keep your hand in, if you are planning for the future, is to spend the same amount of time on actual composition — of whatever you please, however short or nonsensical — that you spend on taking notes and dreaming. (Once you are accustomed to doing it, this side activity can be just as much fun.) In this way you *stay* a writer, just as the person who keeps running stays a runner, thereby preparing yourself far more effectively for your long project than the person with ten volumes of notes and no immediate creative experience in her fingertips.

MEETING AND SETTING DEADLINES

Proposals and outlines, promises of books to be, are often associated with deadlines. Imaginative writers — as distinct from journalists and writers-to-order — respond in wildly differing ways to this type of constraint, which represents an outer-world demand placed on their inner-world activities. One of literary history's severest deadlines was successfully met by Dostoyevsky, who in a scant four months was forced to write an entire novel of approximately five hundred pages (*The Gambler*) while completing an equally long one (*Crime and Punishment*), or forfeit the rights to all his previous works to an unscrupulous publisher. (He dictated both books, one in the morning and one in the afternoon, to a stenographer who became his second wife.)

Here the stentorian voice of the "professional," for whom writing is the sole source of income, intrudes to announce that he or she has done the equivalent all of his or her writing life — two or more projects at the same time, nine to five every day with nary a skip, and, as the ultimate badge of honor, "never missed a deadline once." This attitude, that a writing block or an inability to meet deadlines is the mark of an amateur, has been expressed by the prolific Anthony Burgess: "I can't understand the American literary block . . . unless it means that the blocked man isn't forced economically to write . . . and hence can afford the luxury of fearing the critics' pounce on a new work as not as good as the last (or first)."

Yet outside the market world of work-to-order — whether it is a novel commissioned from an already successful writer or merely a press release or interoffice memo — deadlines, though equally real, are a different sort of animal. Paradoxically, many writers of the same aggressively professional orientation as Burgess find themselves unable to function without a strict timetable externally imposed on them. Their very professionalism has, in effect, infantilized them, leaving them unable to strike out in a completely new direction. A contract must be signed, the marketplace must mandate their fancies, before they feel licensed to begin. Journalists and others who write for a living thus find the transition to imaginative writing — where several years must be devoted to a project with no guarantee of its eventual publication — insuperably difficult to make.

The nebulous world where most art is produced has no contracts and no deadlines other than those the writer sets for himself. Making a successful adaptation to this world means that the writer must determine immediately which of the two camps he belongs to, the deadline needers or the deadline dreaders. Some writers, such as those just mentioned, cannot produce at all unless a deadline looms on the horizon. Others freeze at the slightest hint of outside pressure. Whichever camp you belong to, it makes sense to try, as much as possible, to order your writing environment according to what you know about your own limitations.

If you are a deadline dreader who must actually produce a work by a given date, you should try to start on it early enough to maintain the illusion of working under no deadline at all — or, if the deadline is extremely tight, give serious thought to the advisability of committing yourself to it at all. You must respect your unconscious rhythms enough to give them all the space they need to operate. Trying to force your unconscious partner to produce within a time frame it cannot manage may result in a tremendous block.

Conversely, if you are incapable of writing *anything* without an externally imposed time limit, it makes sense to manufacture your own deadlines in situations where they don't already exist. This can be done by announcing a finish date to other interested parties, such as your agent or publisher, or by deciding to enter your work in a competition. Once the deadline has been externalized in this fashion, you are free to believe it is a binding commitment. You have authorized yourself, indirectly, to begin.

What if — regardless of your deadline orientation — you have committed to a deadline that you believed was possible to meet when you agreed to it but now find yourself unable to proceed? The first thing you must do is inquire of your unconscious whether it is taking umbrage at something intrinsic to the piece of writing or merely at the deadline. This is an important distinction, because the answer must be your guide in deciding which of two courses to take: to extend the deadline or to rethink and reapproach the whole project. Unless you have a trusting and easy relationship with that side of yourself, however, ascertaining this simple information can be hard to do. You will be so busy calling yourself unprofessional that you will not be able to hear the lower-pitched inner voice that is attempting to explain the real problem.

ANNOUNCING INTENTIONS

> There is in the air about a man a kind of congealed jealousy. Only let him say he will do something and that whole mechanism goes to work to stop him.
> — JOHN STEINBECK

Telling the world about a deadline as a means of kicking yourself into gear is one kind of writerly tactic; telling the world everything else about the project can produce a lethal block. Though announcing one's literary plans usually involves the spoken rather than the written word, it is an activity closely related to taking notes. Like notetaking, it is part of the preparatory ritual intended to calm a writer's inner anxiety — or panic — about jumping off the cliff. Nevertheless, talking about a work in or about to be in progress often serves only to distance the writer even further from the act of composition. Eileen Simpson, a writer and wife of John Berryman, makes this testimony about a long poem Berryman planned to write:

> He talked about it so much I suspected he was willing it into being, for I had learned that the chances of a project coming to fruition were in inverse proportion to the amount he discussed it. This was especially true if the talk was high-keyed,

and, to my ears, forced, which meant to me that it was make-work, busy-work, anxiety-relieving work — always plausible, always interesting to hear about; not, however, the real thing.

Of this habit (and what writer has not indulged in it at some point?) Anne Tyler, a writer who "cannot bear to hear people talk about their writing," said: "If they're talking about a plot idea, I feel the idea is probably going to evaporate. I want to almost physically reach over and cover their mouths and say, 'You'll lose it if you're not careful.'"

Some writers, of course, can spill the beans before, during, and after writing their project, with no noticeable adverse effects. Once again, it is up to the individual writer to determine her own specific limits and preferences. When does the outline become the Outline, and at what point does describing a project to others replace the "real thing"? That there is such a point is indisputable, and where that point lies will be different for each writer.

BREAKING OUT OF JAIL

Whether you are announcing your intention to the world at large or only to yourself via your notes, you must be aware of the moment when you cross the line from true preparation to out-and-out stalling. Now it may be that your unconscious has a valid reason for stalling; some unresolved emotional or technical impasse connected with the piece you have conceived makes you not quite ready to carry it to full term. In such a case, you must be flexible enough to heed the block and set your notes aside *before* you overwork them. This way they will be fresh when the time comes to sit down and do the real creative work.

But what if you have passed this point already? What if you have inadvertently gone too far with your notes, so that they now imprison you? How can you break out of jail?

Some ideas may have sat in the notebook too long for rescue; frozen in amber, they are best interred with a quiet prayer as your imagination turns to something fresh and exciting it can explore directly, without the intervening screen of written plans. Other potential works may be salvageable from their note prisons. The first step is to *dis*organize your plan, immediately. Put the notes away. Real control addicts will find this terribly hard to do; they are afraid that if they let go of the edge of the swimming pool, they will drown in three feet of water. So if you can't quite stand to put the notes away, mess them up. Spread a little chaos into your plans; it can produce wonderful results. You have probably tried to nail down too much; now you must let some of it go. Simplify and unstructure your notes. Get rid of those Roman numerals. Use images or actual sentences from the projected piece as your anchor points instead of analytical comments *about* the characters, action, scenery, etc. Best of all, write the first sentence of the real work.

You will discover, once you begin actually writing the piece, how much closer you have moved to the mysterious living center of your story-to-be by imagining it and dwelling inside it instead of describing it from the outside looking in. Moreover, you now have something down on paper that requires no translation from the analytical mode to the imaginative mode; you have taken the first steps down the road of discovery that constitutes the act of art.

Many writers need no more incentive to start than this. Others still prefer to work out the action and structure in some detail before beginning. Either way, it is still impossible — and undesirable — to anticipate everything, least of all the texture and final impact of the work. If you are a prisoner of your notes, you may find that it is far safer *not* to capture every last detail before you begin to write; otherwise you cheat yourself of spontaneous discoveries. (Many novels, for example, fail because their authors kept their characters in the lock-step formation of a prior plan; no merciful writing block rose to allow them to reconsider a too rigid preconception.)

Start dismantling the rational superstructure now, even if

the work you are writing is expository rather than imaginative. The creative process — as distinct from the content of your subject — demands a little unreason to work properly. When your orderly, lifeless notes are in sufficient shambles, your unconscious will stop being bored and the potential work of art they have suffocated will come alive again. Then you'll be ready to start the real adventure, full of pratfalls, tours de force, surprises, frustrations, and unexpected pleasures.

9

Writing over the Block,
Obsessive Rewriting

❖

What I write at the moment turns too much in a tightened
circle. I am feeding off my own substance, and do not renew
myself.

— GÉRARD DE NERVAL
Letter to George Bell

Stories die of their own accord, the Demon said. They are like
us; they want to live, no matter how badly they are treated.

— WILLIAM T. VOLLMAN
"The Grave of Lost Stories"

IN THE BREATHLESS pause between plan and execution,
a little breach opens that quickly widens into a gulf when
the writer stops to look down — and with each added moment
of hesitation the gulf yawns wider and wider. This is the critical point when many take up their notes or dreams again and
return to their safe camps in the realm of possibility, never to
venture back to the edge again. Others, realizing that hesitation will only make the transition harder, strive to keep their
momentum up, jump over the gap, and begin their work. Still
others, gazing into the abyss, know in their hearts they are not
ready but force themselves, sweaty-handed, to pole-vault over

their own reservations and take up their burden on the other side. And a burden it proves to be — nothing in the act of art seems to come naturally, and the results are forced, congealed, unpleasing to make and unpleasing to contemplate.

Norman Mailer has described this last experience:

> Writing at such a time [against one's inclinations] is like making love at such a time. It is hopeless, it desecrates one's future, but one does it anyway because at least it is an act. Such writing is almost unsprung. It is reminiscent of the wallflower who says, "To hell with inhibitions, I'm going to dance." The premise is that what comes out is valid because it is the record of a mood. . . . If you can purge it, if you get sleep and tear it up in the morning, it can do no more harm than any other bad debauch.

Not all writers have the honesty to admit this about some of their work. An alarmingly high percentage of the works produced by writers after they became well known are abortive, unrealized concoctions that would never have been published if their authors were still obscure. This happens not from any conscious conspiracy to dupe the reading public but from the special pressures exerted on the famous to live up to external expectations, a phenomenon I will examine in a later chapter. For now it is enough to say that a whole category of writing exists that has come into being *over* the block, out of a forced act of will power. In these cases, unfortunately, the block has not been strong enough to prevent the act of writing.

Why "unfortunately"? Because making art isn't in every case an act superior to not making art. That belief comes out of the same production-quota mentality that most writers adopt at any moment in their lives when they are not actually producing something. Yet forcing one's way through a block via a kind of internal Sherman's march is not always synonymous with artistic victory. By overriding a real resistance, the writer may be prematurely tearing the curtains away from a delicate, half-formed something not ready for the full light of consciousness.

It takes time for an imaginative idea to grow to full term in the unconscious; how much time depends on how easily it lends itself to expression in words — how pliable the whole relation with the unconscious is — when the writer sits down to compose. If the writer habitually does not listen to his internal signals but proceeds entirely by ego command, he is likely to be insensitive to the requirements of this mostly invisible gestation period. Such a writer will make twenty forced false starts where a more self-trusting writer will have the patience to wait and then know instinctively when the day has arrived for his project to emerge into the light of day.

Here again, only the finest line exists between active, creative waiting and malingering. In some situations it's appropriate to give yourself a tiny kick in the pants to jump over the gap; in other cases you must have the honesty to admit that you do not feel wholly ready or that there is something not quite right about the project itself. Each time the writer faces an entirely different situation and an entirely different solution. *Surrendering* and *listening,* the only real ways out of the dilemma, are impossible acts to perform if you remain locked in a solipsistic master-slave struggle for control over yourself.

How often have you heard someone — or yourself — announce, "Tomorrow I'm going to sit down and *try* to write"? The very way this sentiment is expressed signals that an inner conflict regarding writing versus not writing is going on and that the person has decided to "take herself in hand" by forcing the issue. Self-commands of this sort are fine for the unconflicted but risky for the chronically blocked. For the latter group, a more cautious, less confrontational way of sneaking up on the problem would be to say, "Tomorrow I'm going to sit down and see what happens. If I start the new project, fine. If I don't seem to be able to, perhaps there's something else I could begin, just to be doing something."

When you sit down in the spirit of *trying* to write (as opposed to allowing yourself to write) and actually do manage, in the face of strong resistance, to come up with something, how do you feel afterward? Excited and pleased? Or merely grimly relieved that the dreaded chore has been accomplished, one way or another? If you feel the second way, the quality of your writing may well mirror your inner resentments and ambivalence about being forced to do it. What you do write should always give you at least a small amount of pleasure or satisfaction. If it does not, you may have been exerting only your will and not your full talent.

But, the objection runs — here the chorus of the "pros" interrupts — isn't exerting will what creative discipline is all about? Isn't the ability to sit down to write every day, regardless of mood, the mark of the real writer? Isn't it a beginner's fallacy to believe that one must wait to be "inspired"? Haven't we all been taught that genius is nine-tenths perspiration and one-tenth inspiration? How am I going to perspire if I don't get busy and start to work?

The answers are not simple and, as always, they hinge on the specific situation and writer. Many writers remain erratic in their habits well into professional maturity, following a more tortuous but no less valid path to composition than those who work steadily. A striking example is Philip Larkin, who by his own calculation composed at the rate of three poems a year. This is "the 'beginning late and long choosing' of genius, the crabwise approach to perfection," as Cyril Connolly, a self-confessed blocked writer, put it. Only a small minority, it should be noted, are prolific right from the start. (I will discuss some extreme examples of the logorrheics in a later chapter.)

If you are blocked at any stage in your writing career, the reasons for your resistance must be satisfactorily resolved before you can move ahead and start perspiring; you cannot leapfrog a single stage in your creative development. This natural brake is a great blessing because it compels you to tame an overeager will that must learn painfully and slowly how to adapt itself to the deeper requirements of the psyche.

The key, of course, is to measure yourself against yourself, not against others. Whether you are in the first years of your writing career or at any other stage, there is no reason that you should torture yourself with comparisons to other writers and their output. Your whole attention should be focused not on what you *ought* to be doing but on those unforced patterns of composition that seem to be emerging of their own accord from your unconscious. If you can make this kind of early surrender to yourself and your deepest creative needs for expression, the chances of your being blocked greatly diminish. Equally, your chances of enjoying a steady, uninterrupted flow of composition ten years down the road greatly increase.

Surrender, not control, as Delacroix said, is always the path. It is only when that hidden, inaccessible side of you says yes that you can safely proceed with writing. When your will senses an impenetrable block rising and you have gently tested a number of ways around it, none of which has worked, you must accept a temporary halt and knock at the door of another project — and keep knocking at doors all over the neighborhood until someone lets you in. If, instead, you stubbornly remain at the locked door in front of you, to huff and puff and blow it down, you will enter an empty house — your imagination, the spirit of your endeavor, will have long since fled in dismay.

If you have been writing for a number of years and your block is chronic, you must be prepared to accept your condition totally, as opposed to railing against yourself or forcing out of yourself a kind of inadequate, low-level writing that gives you no pleasure. (This dead matter, again, should be kept distinct from work that your ego may judge as low level but that *does* give you pleasure, works you were meant to write rather than loftier works you *ought* to have written.) You must, in short, give up your dreams of that instant miraculous transformation, always just around the corner, and surrender to the block.

For once, try being deliberate and direct — be conscious — in your decision not to write, instead of letting your unconscious do the work for you. Take responsibility, as they say, for not writing. Quit forcing and stop writing. Give the block a chance to speak to you. This act of surrender, if performed wholeheartedly, should cause you to experience, briefly, some

real relief — and a few surprises about the authentic direction
your talent wants to take.

OBSESSIVE REWRITING

A first novel is like a first pancake; you have to throw it out.
— ANONYMOUS

Forced writing often leads to another kind of nonwriting —
namely, the compulsion to rework projects to death. As a delaying tactic that keeps the writer from embarking on a new
adventure, obsessive rewriting is a highly effective manifestation of the block. Like taking notes, it is something to be let go
of in order to get on with the real work.

Letting go of rewriting must be distinguished from the habit
of junking a promising work (like the schoolboy who torched
his airplane drawing) because you lack the patience or the skill
to complete your project. Here I refer to the tendency to kill a
living work by repeated surgery, amputations, transplants, and
the like under the merciless glare of your analytical (not creative) attention. After many tries you, the mad scientist, produce
a patchwork monster that bears little resemblance to your original conception. And, half-consciously recognizing that you
have created a golem, you must struggle with the compulsive
temptation to continue the revision in a vain attempt to recapture what has been lost. But it is too late. The work, like pastry
dough or a watercolor many times corrected, has been over-
handled. Consider at least the possibility of putting it aside
and moving on.

Some writers, especially beginners, stumble here. They
cannot let go, cannot accept that reworking will never change
a sow's ear into a silk purse. They are determined to *will* the
defunct project back to life by more extreme but essentially
water-treading measures, such as retelling a story in the present tense rather than the past, picking out a minor character
and presenting the whole thing through that person's eyes —
the possibilities for stalling in this manner are endless. Another

year or two passes in which the quality of the writing experience comes to resemble not a master jeweler polishing a diamond, but a cat torture-killing a mouse.

An archetypal case: A young man lives in the country, writing stories and novels while supporting himself as a carpenter and odd-job man (for urbanites, substitute taxi driver). It is a lonely, difficult life with no worldly rewards, not even the basic validation of seeing his works in print. He is a talented writer, but many other equally talented writers are competing with him for the pitifully few outlets of publication. Moreover his works, while competent, lack a certain something — spirit? technique? — to carry them the full distance into art. Aware that this something always eludes him, he relentlessly pursues it through the holy rite of revision. In fact, composition, for our carpenter-author, has come to play more and more a subsidiary role as he endlessly toys with each word he has written. He keeps a tattered copy of his novel by his side wherever he goes, proof to the world that he really is a writer, not a carpenter — but also in case the quintessential new word or phrase should suddenly come to him. What really eludes him, though, is the freshness of effort brought about by a constant assault on the unknown. By clinging to the relics of his writing past, he is traveling in the opposite direction from artistic growth.

Many writers do work in a compulsive fashion, creeping ahead only with the greatest reluctance. This habit of holding on to the past sometimes maddens its sufferers. Why, *why* can't they simply dash off one story or chapter after another, the way so-and-so does? For some, a glacierlike pace turns out to be a natural rate of development, which no power on earth can speed up or alter. It is, however, still development. Obsessive rewriting that goes beyond these limits is *arrested* development, and is to be avoided, especially in the first few years of writing. One is clinging to the meager, lifeless comforts of the mechanical to avoid jumping into the spontaneous.

At some point during their revision of a work, most writers experience a distinct feeling of closure. The obsessive reviser *never* experiences closure. The piece exists in a permanent unhealthy symbiosis with its author. Psychologically, this lack of closure functions in the same way as not writing anything at all, or writing only in fragments — for you can never be judged for what you have not finished. This impasse represents an incubation period that goes on too long. As we saw in Chapter 7, the creative womb exerts a powerful backward pull on all sorts of writers who keep postponing their entry into the world of completed (therefore finite and limited) works — whether they are an "eternal child" who imagines everything and writes nothing, a notetaker who writes an outline instead of a book, or an obsessive rewriter who, like many house remodelers, refuses to acknowledge that the end must finally come.

A writer who finds herself still tied to a work she could have just as easily set aside years ago may want to take a closer look at underlying reasons that have nothing to do with writing. Sometimes the failure to let go may arise only from fear of moving on into the unknown — but other compelling factors may also be at work, as in the classic example of the first novel about a failed first marriage, where an emotional tie above and beyond technical or artistic problems keeps the author joined to the stillborn work. (Gore Vidal has remarked of American novels that they are "autobiographies, usually composed to pay off grudges.")

An extreme reaction to such an insight into your own work is typically to say, "Right! Not only this book but this whole episode in my life was sick!" and toss the manuscript into a blazing fire. For some, such a drastic separation may bring relief, but my own instinct is that this is more master-slave behavior. By destroying the manuscript you are *forcing* closure — and how! Afterward, in calmer moments, you are likely to experience strong grief and regret at the violence you have inflicted on yourself. What is wrong with simply putting the manuscript aside? If you can manage to leave it alone, the passage of time may provide the closure you are unable to give it. Reading it years later, you will have a much sharper perspective on its merits and demerits. Once you destroy it, however, you will have lost forever any opportunity for perspective.

And once you have put this flogged horse away, here is a further piece of advice that is based squarely on the principle that humans are unable to take their pleasures straight. Allow yourself the fun and freedom of starting a new work — nothing as important as the picked-over masterpiece, of course. Tell yourself you're just killing time while saving up energy for that one last rewrite. Tell yourself you *ought* to be hacking away at the rewrite right now (this is a good way to guarantee you won't do it), but for once you are going to indulge yourself by fooling around with something new. The results may surprise you.

Finally, we should never forget that assiduous rewriting, as part of the drive for perfection, is a godlike curse because it is also the means to full consummation of the artist's vision. The vice of obsessive revision can be turned to advantage in matters of style. When asked how often he rewrote a piece, the humorist S. J. Perelman replied that he averaged about thirty-seven times: "I once tried doing thirty-three, but something was lacking, a certain — how shall I say — *je ne sais quoi*. On another occasion, I tried forty-two versions, but the final effect was too lapidary."

There is the story of the guard in a French museum who intervened in horror as an elderly white-bearded gentleman whipped out a paintbrush and began to deface a priceless Monet. It was the artist himself (with a friend as watchdog), indulging in a final revision.

1 0

Forcing Talent into the Wrong Mold

———— ❖ ————

I started writing poetry when I was six and stopped when I was
twenty-six because it was getting a little better, but not terribly
much. When I was fifteen I wrote seven hundred pages of an
incredibly bad novel. . . . Then, when I was nineteen I wrote a
couple hundred pages of another novel, which wasn't very good
either. I was still determined to be a writer. And since I was a
writer, and here I was twenty-nine years old and I wasn't a very
good poet and I wasn't a very good novelist, I thought I would
try writing a play, which seems to have worked out a little better.

— EDWARD ALBEE

AMONG THE various ways writers can force creative energy into a sterile corner is by imposing a whole false
writing persona, whether of style or genre or voice, on themselves. The way out of this impasse involves the difficult task
of discovering your true identity as a writer — a lifelong, constantly evolving process with no guideposts except blind instinct to tell you when you are on the right track. In this
context, writer's block serves as a lie detector test that deter-
mines whether you are forcing yourself down a particular path
for reasons of ego and/or others' advice or example and/or
money, or are writing out of deepest sincerity. Moreover, even
what is sincere can raise questions if your conscious and unconscious selves have diametrically opposed notions about

what direction your writing should take. In time, their dis-
agreement will make itself known in the form of a substantial
block.

This is another version of the battle of *ought* versus *want*
discussed in Chapter 4. In the classic *ought* bind, you have
constructed in your mind a long list of what sorts of things you
ought to be writing and how your career ought to go, to the
point where your self-demands have effectively estranged you
from your true sources of inspiration and creative pleasure.
Whole writing lifetimes have been bent out of shape and tragically sacrificed on the altar of *ought.* It is a special brand of
suicide that can be performed by writing beneath, above, or
even alongside the real current of your imagination.

Examples include the esoteric writer who deliberately attempts a "breakthrough" book to reach a mass audience, or
the children's book author who feels she should "grow up"
and write an adult novel. Now there are numerous cases of
writers who made just such crossovers as these and found
themselves immensely liberated. When the decision is made
either cynically or divorced from one's natural writerly inclinations, however, its essential falseness is thrown back in the
author's face by means of a major block. The short story writer
Katherine Anne Porter, prodded by her editor (on the principle that bigger is better) to write a novel, labored twenty years
to produce *Ship of Fools;* it was a form she ultimately admitted
she did not feel comfortable with. By the same token, a writer
who clings to a mode he has outgrown because it carries a
higher worldly value than the mode he is truly drawn to — a
novelist who yearns for the liberating fantasy of children's literature, to reverse the example — will also find it hard to function in the form he continues to imprison himself within.

Beginning writers with serious aspirations who experience
tremendous difficulty getting their work published often fall
victim to a tempting illusion: if only they can whip out a com-
mercially popular book of some sort — thriller, mystery, romance, even pornography — they will have bought themselves
precious time for their "real" writing. A strange thing may

happen when a young (or middle-aged) writer decides to take what seems to be an eminently practical, worldly-wise step: he may find to his surprise that he has a natural facility in one of these areas — in fact, a greater facility than for his earlier, "serious" experimental efforts, and, having let go the false snobbery that kept him chained to inappropriate forms, he will have discovered his true mode of expression.

On the other hand, such a writer, if he proves successful in his new commercial persona, may have done nothing else but throw himself into another prison, this time a lifelong one. For an inescapable truth emerges here: we are what we write. Someone who writes formulaic entertainments "only" to pay the bills is still a writer of entertainments, no matter what else she does in the rest of her writing time. In one of those mysterious flip-flops of fate, such a writer may find her temporary costume has frozen to her body; once she has tasted the money and recognition her new skill brings her, she cannot return to her original mode.

On the third (and possibly best) hand, the writer who attempts a change of persona solely for expedience may find herself hopelessly blocked. She makes the interesting discovery that it is just as hard to write popular fiction as it is to write anything else. Commercial formula fiction is constructed according to an intricate set of rules that may seem technically difficult — far more difficult, to a certain kind of artist, than what she may be used to writing. Nine times out of ten, the thriller or romance lies half finished on the desk, a casualty not only of the nuts-and-bolts facility it takes to put one of these books together but of the writer's inner conflicts as well. That playful spirit her imagination doesn't find the writing of entertainments an entertaining experience.

Many writers commit this great mistake: they assume that writing commercial fiction is easier than writing "literature." Both in technique and in spirit, it is not. It is simply the mode in which some writers can find exuberant expression and some cannot. For someone not meant to write it at all, the results can be grotesque. Moreover, the works of the most successful popular writers are often themselves naïve and badly constructed. What sets them apart is an indefinable aura of sincerity that their readers unconsciously respond to. These writers *believe* in what they're writing, and they are supported in their belief by the full power of mass marketing. In their work they have found the perfect vehicle for their deepest convictions about life and their personal finances alike. It stands to reason, then, that if you cynically take up one genre when your true talent lies in another, you will never do it as effectively as the "naturals" do. You may grow to do it competently, but paradoxically you may never shine in the popular eye the way a much less skilled writer can — unless you come to believe in it, too. Conversely, if popular fiction or screenplay writing draws you more powerfully than any other type of literature, you are mistaken to feel you must strive to write any "higher" than you naturally do. It is always easier to be yourself as a writer than to sell out in either direction.

Remember, finally, that bending yourself into unnatural poses as a writer is just as likely to occur in the higher realms of literary pursuit as it is in popular or commercial literature. It is entirely possible to prostitute yourself *up* as well as *down;* many serious writers live as much of a double life as the crassest manipulator of the bestseller racket. Like those readers who proudly display their gold-stamped sets of the great classics but secretly cherish paperback mysteries, such writers often show an unconscious split between ego and true inclination. Of this artistic double life Jorge Luis Borges has said:

> I have known many poets . . . who have written well — very fine stuff — with delicate moods and so on — but if you talk with them, the only thing they tell you is smutty stories or speak of politics in the way that everybody does, so that really their writing turns out to be a kind of sideshow. They had learned writing in the way that a man might learn to play chess or to play bridge. They were not really poets or writers at all. It was a trick they had learned, and they had learned it thoroughly.

Another arena in which false identity cards are available to the writer is restricted to the North American literary milieu.

Here is a typical case: As your first assignment in a college creative writing class, you submit a diffuse, ornately written mystical narrative whose parts and subparts you have thoughtfully marked out for your readers with Roman numerals and letters. The instructor, a neo-realist in the grand tradition of American truck-stop regionalism, pounces like a tiger, eagerly followed by the rest of the class. You are informed, gently or ruthlessly, that real art consists of clean, spare, "seamless" prose and not your kind, which he finds outrageously Swinburneian — and that is not even taking into account the Roman numerals. Following the example of several microgenerations of good-intentioned creative writing teachers, he advises you to write instead about "what you know best" — that is, your immediate external environment — just like your fellow apprentice cabinetmakers, who are dutifully cannibalizing their lives and loves to produce identically crafted prose pieces. Or they may confuse real life with lowlife and turn out stories of hitchhikers and hookers and rural Gothicism that are actually far more romantic, in their way, than anything in the *Thousand and One Nights.*

Now it must be said that there is an 80 percent probability that your instructor is dead right about your present mode of writing — it *is* awful — and that you have received what you came to the class to get, namely, good advice and instruction. But in the other ineffable 20 percent of the cases, he will be wrong and you will be right, because those ponderous sentences, as full of seams as a hand-sewn fin-de-siècle fancy dress, are actually your voice, or the beginnings of your voice, or the beginnings of *one* of your voices (the single voice itself being another questionable sacred cow).

How do you know who is really right in this situation? By a simple test. If you have only been imitating, you will find the transition to a different style (though not necessarily the instructor's favored kind) relatively easy, and a relief. The change will excite you and expand your sense of artistic possibilities. If, however, you have been writing out of the core of your as yet unformed artistic abilities, you will find any alteration grating and unnatural. Like a lefty being forced to write right-handed, you will constantly backslide into your old ways, and your public efforts to please your audience (instructor and classmates) with a "simple" style will be even more artificial than your original work. Here writer's block is an eloquent expression of that side of you which stubbornly refuses to write out of character, no matter how much outside pressure is brought to bear.

Why try to be what you think you should be as a writer, when discovering with humility what you are, no matter how unpleasant this news may be to your ego (I am a sporadic writer, I am a writer who will never be taught in a literature class, I am a writer whose work is out of step with fashion), carries so much more inner resonance, both with yourself and with your readers? The vast majority of cases of writer's block examined in this book can be labeled healthy, instinctive reactions to an attempt at *self-falsification* — whether you are trying to live up to a self-image as a perfect writer, a poet-prophet of your time, an eight-hour-a-day writer, or whatever. Every writer has within herself a certain setpoint, a natural and unconscious home base, from which the conscious identity is built. If you have the courage to set aside the false self-image and simply let the writing be what it wants to be, the block is likely to go away.

A tremendous energy is released when you let go, even temporarily, some of those superficial ambitions and find out for yourself how you prefer to write. For once, take the opportunity to lose your self-consciousness and do not worry, on one hand, if what you are writing captures the spirit of the times or, on the other, is what the market, high or low, wants. Just as there is no longer a debtor's prison, there is likewise no writer's prison either — except the one we construct for ourselves. You don't *have* to write any way at all; *you can write any way you please.* Here Rilke's advice to the young writer goes equally well for the blocked writer:

> It makes no difference what one writes as a very young person, just as it makes almost no difference what else one undertakes. The apparently most useless distractions can be a pretext for inwardly collecting oneself. . . . One may do *anything;* this alone corresponds to the whole breadth life has. But one must be sure not to take it upon oneself out of opposition, out of spite toward hindering circumstances, or, with others in mind, out of some kind of ambition.

The sentiment that Rilke expresses is neither impractical nor too high flown; it is the basis of all creative endeavor. As we have seen again and again, writers who are seriously and chronically blocked are usually out of touch not only with the simple, the innocent, and the playful but with their own identity. They need to go back to square one and take their first stumbling steps again, suspending all sophisticated judgment and creative self-directives until they have reestablished genuine contact with their inner sources.

But what if you feel genuinely trapped in your present mode of writing and want to make a break? What if you are experiencing a block in your attempts to leap from the confining but comfortable known to the terrifying unknown? This situation of *authentic* change of writing roles deserves to be examined more closely.

CHANGING THE WRITING PERSONA

Some years ago the journalist Tom Wolfe was faced by a "notes that refuse to make a story" block that proved to mask a deeper creative dilemma. Sent to cover a hot rod and custom car show by the *New York Herald Tribune,* he had dutifully turned in "exactly the kind of story any of the somnambulistic totem newspapers in America would have come up with."

Wolfe knew that something else was going on, but it was more than just a different story — inside him a whole new way of looking at the world was struggling to emerge. The conflict between this surge of creativity and his commitment to old-fashioned journalese produced a massive writing block.

Fascinated by the custom cars as a form of new proletarian art, Wolfe followed up the story in California for *Esquire* magazine but found himself unable to write the second story in the usual way. Back in New York, he sat hopelessly over his typewriter and finally called Byron Dobell, the managing editor of *Esquire,* to confess defeat. Dobell instructed Wolfe to type his notes for someone else to write up.

> So about 8 o'clock that night I started typing the notes out in the form of a memorandum that began, "Dear Byron." I started typing away, starting right with the first time I saw any custom cars in California. I just started recording it all, and inside of a couple of hours, typing along like a madman, I could tell that something was beginning to happen. By midnight this memorandum to Byron was twenty pages long and I was still typing like a maniac. . . . I wrapped up the memorandum about 6:15 A.M., and by this time it was 49 pages long. I took it over to *Esquire* as soon as they opened up, about 9:30 A.M. About 4 P.M., I got a call from Byron Dobell. He told me they were striking out the "Dear Byron" at the top of the memorandum and running the rest of it in the magazine.

The result (for good or ill) was "The Kandy-Kolored Tangerine-Flake Steamline Baby," a bit of journalistic history. Wolfe's description of this breakthrough into a style uniquely his own is an eloquent statement of the suffering one endures when trying to write against the grain of one's nature — and the indescribable relief experienced when one lets go the inhibitions and the *shoulds.* That click, that feeling of release that comes with what the novelist Lynn Freed calls "hitting the voice," is always essential, regardless of what your ego or the current wisdom may be saying. Wolfe had been locked into the confines of the traditional magazine story, which had suited neither him nor his subject. Heeding the block meant having the courage to move in another direction, though in Wolfe's case this was a spontaneous and unconscious act born of desperation rather than a deliberately thought-out decision.

Writers often move on to a new genre while still working in their original forms. Of this experience, the poet May Sarton has said:

> Sometimes the demon of self-doubt comes to tell me that I've been fatally divided between two crafts, that of the novel and that of poetry, but I've always believed that in the end it was the total work which would communicate a vision of life and it really needs different modes to do that. . . . In the novel or the journal you get the journey. In a poem you get the arrival.

Similarly, the novelist Gina Berriault found writing one-act plays a tremendous lift of spirit because in them she discovered a freer manner of expression not available to her in short stories, a way of cutting loose from the prison of crafting perfect sentences and perfect paragraphs. In her stage-writing persona, she found herself able to enter her characters' lives with greater abandon than she could in her novels and stories. If her stories represent Rilke's "innermost," she concludes, then the plays are most definitely her "outermosts"; together they embrace a wider vision than either form taken separately.

Discovering who one is as a writer at any given time in a writing life can be an experience that causes a major upheaval, even to the point of changing from poetry to drama (Albee, above), from novels to poetry (Thomas Hardy), from fiction to journalism (Norman Mailer, Truman Capote). Human nature being what it is, however, many writers unhappy with who they *really* are nourish daydreams of being quite a different sort of writer. Unsatisfied with *The Mikado*, Sir William Gilbert wanted desperately to be a writer of great stage tragedies, a task for which he, an inspired comedy librettist, was entirely unsuited. Similarly, writers who have spent the bulk of their careers in journalism are always announcing that they are about to take up fiction. In these cases, the dream of change is no true goal but an ego ideal — as well as a sneaky way of putting down one's real accomplishments.

In the same way, the mode certain writers regard as their primary accomplishment is not one the world comes to regard as their forte. The richness of personal experience, observation, and opinion, for example, that shine forth in Anaïs Nin's private diaries overshadow the beautifully wrought but rather narrow and solipsistic world of the novellas she believed were her real accomplishment. Then there is the case of Joseph Joubert, a contemporary of Diderot's. Ironically hailed by commentators as an "author without a book, a writer without writings," Joubert discovered that what he had to offer were ideas, without a conventional literary "house" to put them in. He was an inspired aphorist, and the notebooks in which he kept his daily jottings turned out to be the proper and natural medium of his art, despite his friends' urgings that he cast them into some more ambitious and conventional form.

It is a delicate matter to determine whether a new medium is meant for your talents or whether changing into it represents only a compensatory daydream. Usually, the problem takes care of itself in a pragmatic way: what you end up writing the most of is probably what you were "meant" to do — that is, it is what you truly *want* to do. The only way to find out if your talent belongs in a different genre is to make the leap and try. Even if you fall on your face, you will at least have had the satisfaction of exploring that alternate path; you will never again have to wonder if that was really the road you ought to have taken.

How does a writer find the shoe that fits? It may be helpful to commit to paper a statement of the kind of writer you think you are or ought to be. List genre, category, and style. Then look at this description. Does it excite you, or do you feel limited? If you were to start all over again as a writer, would you pick a different or alternate mode of expression? What would it be? Do you have an irresistible desire to try out this mode now, or do you prefer to keep it in the realm of daydream? Have you already made attempts in this direction? In actual practice, which mode gives you the most satisfaction?

Be warned that it's not usually an overnight transformation. A case in point is a certain romance writer who after years of profitably churning out bodice rippers found herself completely blocked, an unmistakable signal of her mounting inner displeasure at formulaic writing. Her way out of the block was to begin a new book that would *not* be a romance. Old habits die hard, though, and the first child of her new freedom was a fascinating creature, neither fish nor fowl. Bodices were half ripped; the rigid plot half deconstructed; characters half developed into three-dimensionality. This writer had clearly obligated herself to write a few more books before she would be securely settled into her new mode — and in the meantime she was going to have to find another way to make her living. This example illustrates the hazards of postponing the switch. If you put off the experiment too long, if you squelch your desire to explore some of the less conventional byways of your psyche, your writing muscles may stiffen in one mode and you may lose the creative flexibility to realize your dream.

It is human nature to resist change. Only when an impassable roadblock suddenly rears up on our accustomed route (or rut) do we ever consider trying another path. That is why writer's block, guiding the writer always away from stagnation toward change and new possibilities, is such a useful, benign, and ultimately blessed instrument of all creative endeavor.

I I

When Society Imposes the False Persona

———— ❖ ————

The public and the private worlds are inseparably connected.
... The tyrannies and servilities of the one are the tyrannies
and servilities of the other.

— VIRGINIA WOOLF

I T IS SELF-EVIDENT that society as well as the individual
writer imposes barriers on expression, but not all writers
or would-be writers, besides those most dramatically affected,
realize how society's sanctions operate as a form of externalized writer's block. Though many might put political censorship at the top of the list of these outer-world blocks, the first
and most basic barrier is economic. Whole groups of people
denied the right to a decent education confront a massive block
to expression that is not of their own making. For the poor of
any race or nation, being on the lowest rung of society's ladder
means, statistically, that far fewer artists have the chance to
emerge and sing. Where education and economic opportunity
are not available, the art of written language, with few exceptions, cannot be practiced.

At the turn of the twenty-first century this is a problem that
has worsened rather than improved in many countries that

count themselves as bearers of civilization. As writers we all carry the consequences of this selective silencing, for a block that shuts out large sections of a population impoverishes and ultimately weakens the whole culture.

A second and more pervasive block, corollary to the first, has to do with cultural and social expectations. This outer-world block — a barrier to publication that can be correspondingly internalized by a sensitive writer — consists of the wide range of censorship, intended or implied, that is exerted on writers by their publishers. This censorship, which in Western democracies is rarely overt or even conscious, extends well beyond the familiar issue of art versus commerce. What it amounts to is a bias against the truly different and the truly new — in subject, in aesthetics, in attitudes, in form or presentation of art.

Until the past two decades the publishing block served to exclude, in both England and North America, a great deal of writing from racial minorities, serious writing from women, and homosexual writing — the last category ghettoized either to small companies who had to consecrate their publishing identities to this literature alone or to avant-garde publishers. The possibility of joining the middle-class, mainstream literature was simply unavailable to writers who were from certain backgrounds or dealt with certain topics.

To some degree this situation has changed, but censorship of sensibility is an ongoing reality and the biases have moved into subtler areas. Now, for example, the pressures are often twofold: outsiders expect a writer who belongs to one of the previously excluded groups to write only about her identified "minority," whatever that may be; equally, she may be expected by those who believe the purpose of art is primarily sociological to present her community to the world in a particular (that is, flattering) light.

This is a no-win situation in which the pressure to create within the framework of newly formed clichés can often become overwhelming. The unconscious reluctance to create the kind of art that both ego and community believe appropriate for a certain writer working at a certain time in a certain medium can produce a massive block. Being put in a category is positive or negative only to the degree that you get to choose that category yourself: if either someone else or your own sense of obligation has crammed you into it, that child of yours may feel as if he's been locked in a new kind of closet.

THE SOCIAL BLOCK THAT LANGUAGE IMPOSES

The dilemma faced by many writers who grew up learning to read and write in the "language of the colonizers" was once addressed by James Baldwin, who said, "You bring your experience to the language, and that changes the language." But as Toni Morrison has pointed out, the problem can be more subtle and more difficult:

> I am a black writer struggling with and through a language that can powerfully evoke and reinforce hidden signs of racial superiority, cultural hegemony, and dismissive "othering" of people and language. . . . The kind of work I have always wanted to do requires me to learn how to maneuver ways to free up the language from its sometimes sinister, frequently lazy, almost always predictable employment of racially informed and determined chains.

The self- and social censorship that occurs in these mental decisions before the act of writing even begins can direct a writer in all sorts of ways, good and bad. The important thing is to remain fully aware both of society's expectations — which will almost always be somewhat cynically determined — and of what you as a writer and a human being are willing to live with. You must know yourself very well before choosing which path you are going to take. Otherwise you will find your unconscious doing the protesting for you.

Here is an example of the barrier that a dominant-language audience can impose. In subcultures where a creole mix or argot is spoken, the writer faces an even more basic problem than that of desensitizing a racially charged language: How do I render dialect faithfully but still intelligibly? Do I write only for fellow speakers or do I aim for a larger audience? This must be a deliberate decision. When he wrote a novella of Maui plantation life, *All I Asking for Is My Body,* Japanese-American writer Milton Murayama said: "I was thinking of the *New Yorker, Harper's,* and the *Atlantic.* I wanted my pidgin to be understood by the editors and readers of those magazines. . . . What I did was three things: use phonetic spelling only on a few words which didn't occur too often, use the syntax and rhythms of pidgin in the dialogue, and use standard English in the narration except for a few pidgin expressions." Despite the entirely accessible language, for many reasons including ethnic and marketing biases the audience for Murayama's little-known classic has been limited mostly to Hawaii. The number of fine books similarly entombed is legion.

Given the fate of Murayama's book, what if you wanted to write your novel entirely in one of the various forms of Hawaiian pidgin? The well-intentioned counsel of others regarding the literary suicide you would be committing might silence you before you began a great and touching masterpiece of the Pacific. Even as you note that famous Anglo writers can publish novels written in impenetrable Caribbean pidgin by virtue of their prior reputation, as a realist you also understand that you, an unknown if genuine pidgin speaker, are unlikely to be given the same opportunity — not just out of unconscious racism and the worship of celebrity, but the more mundane and arbitrary reason that your part of the world is not yet a recognized literary port of call.

Once having made that real-world assessment, you face a difficult choice. If you choose the mainstream road, will you silence a livelier and more authentic voice? If you stay rigidly purist, will you deny yourself an audience or possibly cut off an opportunity to play in an expanded arena of language possibilities? Here there is no right or wrong decision outside an individual writer's self-knowledge and deepest instincts. If, within yourself, you have not come to the point where you trust and respect your own instincts absolutely, you will not be able to make the right choice no matter how well you can articulate your reasons intellectually. As I have said before, the possibility to "sell out" works in two directions. In a situation where social rewards and sanctions are muddied or in transition, the *oughts* on both sides of any literary issue tend to drown out the *wants* unless you stay entirely dedicated to your deepest preferences.

The farther you are from the literary mainstream, the more outrageous the already brutal publishing realities become. And so you must be prepared for a tough struggle against the tendency to silence yourself when you see that the world is not going to accept your vision.

INTERNALIZING THE EXTERNAL BLOCK

One equal-opportunity external barrier that writers of all races, sexes, and dialects face is a subtler form of expectation in art at every level — in the way in which characters are presented, in the way words appear on a page, in density of language, and the hundred other "little" details that add up to formidable conventions of aesthetics and subject.

Breaking free of these bonds is a complicated business that is more likely to bring you external sanctions rather than rewards. To be true to your artistic standards in your work may have the inescapable consequence of denying you an audience — at least temporarily, until tastes change — and this very real consideration may only increase your inner conflicts about beginning an ambitious new work that you sense will not be published. Are you, like van Gogh, going to pour heart and soul into painting after painting that will never be sold, never be seen and appreciated by eyes other than those of their creator? Or are you, at some point, going to "mend your ways" and do what is expected of you?

It is possible for an imagination, in the right vessel, to expand and refine itself. It is also possible to have a rich imagination ruined in the crucible of culture, the personality being so dependent and impressionable it shapes itself in a too-conventional mold. But none of these transformations takes place in a vacuum; all occur within the context of a specific society. It is the writer's responsibility to learn about the hidden assumptions of the culture he or she writes in, because these assumptions determine the actual publication, not to mention reception, of the work. This is a more complicated business than the old adage to "know your audience"; you must know, rather, your intermediaries — those who select the works for publication and determine who their audience will be. Whatever its intrinsic value, an unpublished book is not a book that lives. If you are to exert any control over the selection process yourself, you must be prepared to wage a powerful and informed fight for your work's right to exist.

A writer who knows who she is and how her work fits or does not fit into a current literary milieu can draw from this knowledge the inner confidence to continue if her work is rejected time and again; or is badly published and ignored; or any of the thousand real and irreversible tragedies that can befall a writer's work once it leaves her desk. Most important, because she is fully conscious of the range of often cynical and trend-following decisions in the publishing process, she is more likely to stay her own writerly person and less likely to perform an unconscious act of self-distortion to please her masters — an outcome worse than silence itself. A writer who stays innocent of this process is more likely to believe that her work is no good and will be more susceptible to pressures to write books in a conventional vein. (Of course, bad writers use the vagaries of the publishing world as an excuse, too, which makes the whole business of discrimination and self-appraisal all the more complicated.)

A FEW SIDE BENEFITS OF EXCLUSION: AN HERETICAL NOTE

Considered in the narrow prism of professional recognition and monetary reward, the vast majority of serious writers can be said literally to lead disadvantaged lives. They must hold another job. They must be willing to sacrifice, *for a lifetime,* quotidian status, money, or even recognition in their own field. This is a test of character that most professions don't require of their initiates. In what other vocation can you do your most advanced and difficult work — at the level of, say, a full professor — while holding the position of department secretary (and receiving the equivalent wage)?

In the full knowledge that we are making a virtue of necessity, how can this fact of life be turned from a silencer into an advantage? Consider first of all that, given the inverted values of our society on one hand and the artist's propensity for dangerous inflation on the other, being excluded from the biggest rewards may not be such a terrible fate, and in some cases may even be a psychological lifesaver. Though it may seem mad to say this, lowered expectations can be an advantage to the serious artist and, in the right spirit, can keep the creative environment at its ideal gestating temperature of benign neglect. By the "right spirit" I mean not one of passively accepting or caving in to the social status quo but of making a pragmatic decision to capitalize on whatever opportunities for deeper development marginalization does offer. Since having little money is a reality anyway, an inner decision not to count on large financial rewards or wide recognition means you will be more likely to stay on your own path in this complicated business of writerly unfolding.

For women, the lowered expectations associated with their performance can actually be a valuable adaptive tool in becoming a writer — *vide* the Brontë sisters, toiling quietly as governesses (and writing their novels) while their brother Branwell, the identified genius, fumbled the ball under his father's and society's crushing expectations of male performance. Again, this is not intended as an argument for the status quo, which has already changed somewhat for women; it is simply a pragmatic suggestion for exploiting that preexisting environment of helpful indifference in which to perform the act of art.

The only problem is that, as with all marginalized minorities, a dual inheritance is involved: too often, lowered expectations are accompanied by severely lowered self-esteem. As the writer Evelyn White has pointed out, women can still experience a block in "self" as well as in writing. Because they "are taught that their personal need to write is secondary to the needs of the workplace and their families . . . women cannot hide themselves away from the demands of everyday life in order to write in uninterrupted solitude." And here the challenge becomes that of raising one's esteem, one's sense of owning the right to write, without overinflating expectations at the same time.

It is also helpful, by way of contrast, to consider the important disadvantage that societal superiority gives to men when they decide to be artists. Far more conditioned to equate their self-esteem entirely with worldly advancement and financial reward in their chosen professions, men go through their own kind of culturally induced agonies and abasements in their struggle as artists. They manage to silence themselves very effectively by yielding to the temptation to turn their craft into a vehicle for serious moneymaking when their true inclinations may lie elsewhere. The self-recriminations of a man who sacrificed his desire to be an artist simply to be what society expected — a provider for his family and a financial success — are as deep and bitter as the regrets suffered by a woman who yielded to those same pressures to sacrifice her career in order to support her husband in his.

A long-forgotten scene, twenty-five years old, rises in my memory: two twenty-year-olds, married quickly to accommodate an unexpected baby, struggling in a cheap apartment. The new husband harbors some thoughts — as vague and misty as such thoughts can possibly be at the age of twenty — about being a writer. He wants to go to Paris, wants all three of them to go to Paris, so he can pursue his vague and misty dreams. He sports, tentatively, a beret. The new wife, exhausted, hands a visitor a page of manuscript from a nearby desk. "Look at it! Read it!" she demands, her face contorted with rage. "It isn't any good, is it?" She does not want to go to Paris. She does not think her husband should be writing at all. She thinks he should be concentrating his energy on finding a good job to support her and his child. And to make her point she does not hesitate to shame him in public.

Rigid roles diminish every member of a society. So do the lingering hidden assumptions of republics founded on a slave economy. The deep inequities reach every corner of the land and the heart. Writers who directly or indirectly feel the impact of such social realities must often draw their motivation from a refusal to let outer circumstances overwhelm and silence them. They must make a private affirmation that even though history is the reality we are all condemned to live within, for them and them alone — and with no judgments passed on the decisions of their peers — it will not be an alibi for silence. And out of that knowledge of exclusion, that refusal to accept it, comes a deep reengagement with the writing process.

Finally, it is necessary to mention one of the most frivolous uses of history as alibi, a statement made to me by a blocked (and not coincidentally an alcoholic) poet: "How can anybody write a line at all with the shadow of the H-bomb hanging over us every day?" If that sentiment were really true, the last half century of poetry and other forms of literary endeavor should perhaps be consigned to the garbage can. In contrast to the immediate realities of social exclusion we have been examining, this fact of history, though equally real, seems a bit abstract to function as a trigger for a long-term writer's block. There is sometimes a tendency among artists to avoid the mundane, embarrassing personal explanation when a grand and noble one is also at hand. It does sound better to say one can't write because of the H-bomb (or unnamed artistic torments) than because of a hangover. This lie, whether it is directed to others or to oneself, remains a lie, just as its author remains blocked until he is ready to tell himself the truth.

POSTSCRIPT: COMING LATE TO WRITING

Forgiving yourself means accepting the fact that you will never
have the past of your dreams.

— ANONYMOUS

Women and men whose lives or social obligations (there is, of
course, often no clear distinction) swept them away from writing face a special problem, and a great deal of inner resistance,
when they either return or come new to writing late in life. In
Silences, Tillie Olsen vividly described the block that comes
from long delay or postponement of the writing adventure:

> The habits of a lifetime when everything else had to come
> before writing are not easily broken, even when circumstances
> now often make it possible for writing to be first; habits of
> years — response to others, distractibility, responsibility of
> daily matters — stay with you, mark you, become you. The cost
> of "discontinuity" (that pattern still imposed on women) is
> such a weight of things unsaid, an accumulation of material so
> great, that everything starts up something else in me; what
> should take weeks, takes me sometimes months to write; what
> should take months, takes years.

This is a gloomy and familiar predicament, but it is still not
entirely devoid of hope. First of all, if you are experiencing the
latecomer's sluggishness, comfort yourself with the knowledge
that although a marathon runner might be able to run a two-
mile course in five minutes, it is going to take you considerably
longer because you are out of shape. A person who is out of
shape is in the same boat as a person who has never been in
shape. You cannot impose expectations from a writing past,
when you were fit, onto the present, when you are not.

It takes a certain amount of humility to realize this, but
humility is a far more freeing attitude than the brand of self-
criticism that attacks you for failing to rise immediately to your
former professional standards in writing or in any other area
of your life. If you have left off piano playing for twenty years,

you do not sit down and attempt concert-level Liszt or Brahms. You start with scales, slowly, until your hands begin to remember the way. You must realize that, starting late, you may never reach or regain the technical proficiency required to play Liszt, but what lies within your natural limits you can learn to play well.

The "too late" mentality is an insidious one that feeds seamlessly into writer's block. Yet people are as prone to believing they have missed the boat when they are twenty-three and thirty as they are at age seventy-three. It's purely a state of mind. The magic moment Now has no age, and that is the moment in which each of us is obliged to live. All that exists in this timeless world is the word or sentence you are putting down on paper. Do not look back to what might have been, or forward to what may never happen. Concentrate on the moment of composition.

After you have written your first sentence, go on to the next. Nothing else in the world except you and that sentence has any importance. Remember that your muscles are stiff and must be slowly relaxed, not forced, into the task. Although it may be true that you no longer possess the energy of earlier years or that life has indeed hardened you into attitudes that dam up an easy flow of words, still you possess the supreme advantage that is usually lacking in youth: patience. And patience, patience in all things, is the most valuable quality a writer can have.

12

*Using Writing
to Hide from Life*

——— ❖ ———

You can immerse yourself in the flat white abyss of the page,
hide from yourself in your private universe, which will still
explode and vanish.

— TADEUSZ KONWICKI

THE RELATION between art and life is a topic that provokes a good deal of vague talk about which realm is
preferable or morally superior to the other. Art's practitioners
like to imagine they have the option, when things on earth get
too difficult to bear, to launch their little coracle and sail off to
W. B. Yeats's timeless holy city of the East, where they will
"set upon a golden bough to sing / To lords and ladies of
Byzantium." Unfortunately, for all but the most compulsively
productive, such a tidy escape out of reality — either long term
or only in times of duress — is not a possibility, however much
they might wish it so. Let's explore some of the ultimately
benevolent ways in which creative resistance blocks this "escape route" from life into art.

THE PRODIGY'S DILEMMA

If you take into account that this "author" is eight years old,
you've got to admit he's got an awful lot of talent! Lope de Vega
wrote his first play when he was ten years old — Stas was seven
and a half when he began. If he keeps on at this rate and
continues to write as much, then undoubtedly his works will be
numbered in the thousands.

— STANISLAW IGNACY WITKIEWICZ
artist, boasting of his son of the same name:
future artist, playwright, madman, and suicide

Precocity is a common, if not universal, adjunct to artistic
development. Some youngsters spend their childhood and adolescence engaged in an outpouring of art — stories, poems,
paintings, musical composition — that either ends abruptly
when they reach maturity or leads them very early into a vocation in the arts.

The typical child prodigy grows into an intense, even eccen-
tric young person who often experiences a substantial early
success by virtue of talent, years of precocious training, and
admirable productivity. (It is this last quality, the continuing
steady output of work straight into early adulthood, that most
sharply distinguishes a prodigy from a *puer,* who may have
experienced a similar childhood but, once grown, does not
retain the ability to complete a project.) Those prodigies who
become artists (or rather, who *stay* artists after they have grown
up) share a certain pattern of characteristics, chief of which is
the inescapable fact that their childhoods were sacrificed on
the altar of art. The emotional and social isolation that accompanied their early experience as children engaged in adult
activity marks them for life.

As a late-appearing symptom of this early imbalance, tragically but almost predictably something seems to happen to
prodigies after their impressive start. In one way or another
they hit the wall, often in their late twenties or early thirties,
the true end of adolescence and a time when the lingering
ghost of childhood must be sacrificed to a full maturity. This

is the moment when life presents the industrious, ever-productive prodigy with the emotional bill for his too mature endeavors, which is usually very high.

Paradoxically (and perhaps unfairly), the hard-working prodigy runs a higher risk of experiencing a nervous breakdown than the perennially blocked *puella,* whose drifting ways allow her to elude all the major emotional passages of life. The first sign that an emotional crisis is in the works is an abrupt halt in the steady outpouring of written material. As the prodigy's formidable creative engine runs out of steam, the block can be followed by more drastic consequences. The mysterious misfortunes begin: the emotional problems, the substance abuse, but most of all that crashingly sudden silence.

Why should the prospects for prodigies, seemingly bright, frequently turn out to be so dim? I have said that art is playful — and fantasy is certainly an important and positive element of a happy childhood. Art and fantasy, however, are not synonymous. The artist bears the child as one of many identities. He is not himself a "creative child"; such a one-on-one identification is disastrous to make. And although an early immersion in this monastic and solipsistic discipline often serves a sensitive adolescent as a needed sanctuary in which to hide from the emotional and sexual storms of impending adulthood, to enter too early, and to stay too long, is to miss (at great emotional cost) the transition to an adult sensibility.

But there's another person involved here. Almost every case of striking precocity has a parent behind the scenes, a parent who has attempted the same discipline, a parent who has actively encouraged premature achievement, a parent whom the prodigy has always striven to please. Not surprisingly, possibly the biggest bumper crop of literary prodigies in the Western tradition was produced during the Victorian era, with its intense, even claustrophobic focus on family life. This special brand of domestic religion spawned an alarming number of fragile young genius acolytes, shadow extensions of dominant parents who had not fully realized their own artistic leanings. The mental sufferings of these prodigies in later life were as spectacular as their early achievements. Charles Lamb, Samuel Taylor Coleridge, the Brontës, John Ruskin, John Stuart Mill, Robert Louis Stevenson, the American Margaret Fuller — all these writers, their identities still too heavily bound up with those of their parents, suffered mental crises at the crucial transition from adolescence to adulthood.

Prodigies discover that the wall they hit is nothing other than the outer boundary, the skin, of the parent they grew up inside; they are aging prisoners in a womb that refuses to release them. The self-imprisonment that precocious talent uses to duplicate the parental structure is vividly described in a fictional portrait of a teenage poet by Milan Kundera:

> The poet, banished from the safe enclosure of childhood, longs to go out into the world, but because he is afraid of the real world he constructs an artificial, substitute world of verse. He lets his poems orbit around him like planets around the sun. He becomes the center of a small universe in which nothing is alien, in which he feels everything is constructed out of the familiar materials of his own soul. Here he can achieve everything which is so difficult "outside."

Kundera adds, cruelly, that such a young poet's true interaction with the outside world begins only when everyone laughs at the grandiose emotions of his verses, rudely bursting the amniotic bubble of vanity that envelops him. But if such healing laughter never comes, there is the added penalty of the solitary nature of writing, which can shut an already too sequestered person even farther away from the world.

But now that this arena of all creative activity, all hope of love and reward and identity, has been revealed as a jail cell instead of a sanctuary, what is the poor *Wunderkind* to do? The very young writer is stuck with a devouring technique that has already digested the meager life experiences of its owner and now begins, as it were, to feed off living tissue. John Ruskin, at age eleven writing two-thousand-line poetic commentaries on travels with his parents, by age twelve had written a poem plaintively titled "Want of a Subject." John Stuart Mill complained that the premature cultivation of his intellect by his doting father had left him "stranded at the commencement of my voyage, with a well-equipped ship and a rudder, but no sail; without any real desire for the ends which I had been so carefully fitted out to work for."

And so, in the middle of all this, comes the block. At first it is an occasion of great panic for the prodigy. The foundation of his whole identity, the one thing that has won him praise his whole life, has crumbled. Underlying this apparent calamity, however, is an unconscious but deeply felt protest at having been forced to live the life of a performing seal. A prodigy who suddenly becomes blocked should therefore consider that he may be experiencing a healthy signal from the unconscious — a signal that he needs a respite from being locked up inside himself, that he needs more experience in the world, experience that will wean him (no matter how precociously adult his intelligence) from his emotional babyhood.

As he tells us in "Crisis in My Mental History," John Stuart Mill temporarily stopped writing at age twenty and viewed his silence afterward with relief: "It was of no common importance to me at this period, to be able to digest and mature my thoughts for my own mind only, without any immediate call for giving them out in print. Had I gone on writing, it would have much disturbed the important transformation in my opinions and character, which took place during those years."

The writer's block in such cases — if it is properly interpreted — effectively short-circuits a prolonged escape from and avoidance of life. For the time being, at last, the very young writer is obliged to go out and live her unlived life instead of, in the words of the poet Stephen Shrader, "leaving by the closet door." An artist or a thinker is just as obliged to meet the emotional demands of a lifetime as any other person, and neglects them at her peril.

The proliferation of creative writing programs in North America highlights the precocity problem. Because they are based on a model of academic rather than artistic development, these programs tend to make young people believe that they should be the writerly equivalent of an assistant professor by age twenty-six or so. The early bloomers, initially highly rewarded by this system, find themselves, in their mid- to late twenties, cast utterly adrift, without structure or support, expected on the basis of their first novel or handful of perfect stories (every step of whose production was overseen by a supportive parental figure) to continue progressing "brilliantly" in a discipline in which sustained expression demands the emotional maturity of a much older person. Those who have received a great deal of attention for these early works are particularly under pressure to continue duplicating their efforts. The painful fact that an impenetrable writer's block may force them to face, however, is that these first books of theirs were actually the performing seal's finale; if any future works at all are to be forthcoming, a different person altogether is required to write them. And their most pressing task in life will be to put aside their *Wunderkind* persona (and, for a time at least, their attempts at art) and become that person.

Some prodigies who weather the crisis of young adulthood often abandon fiction or poetry and turn to essay writing, journalism, or criticism, all of which provide a strong rational framework that can support a fragile personality at the same time that they conceal emotional underdevelopment and related conflicts — traits that imaginative writing mercilessly exposes. Expository writing, an honorable profession in its own right, has always been a time-honored detour for the blocked imaginative writer. Late Victorian England, significantly, produced the greatest essayists of English literature from its aging prodigies — but not the greatest art.

The prodigy who heeds the block by *living* may never return to writing if (as in many cases) its main purpose was as a sanctuary or a way to please parents, and if it did not at some level transform itself into a true vocation. If you were or are one of those persons, giving up writing is not failure but an affirmation of your true identity. Do not allow the expectations of others — particularly of family — to make you feel guilty once you have made the decision to stop writing. You are not blocked; you have decided to do something else with your life. In betraying other people's image of you, you have discovered your own.

One reason many prodigies never recover from their creative block in adult life may be unacknowledged rage against a ruined childhood sacrificed to meet a parent's unfulfilled dreams. Many ex-prodigies live out their adult lives in unconscious dedication to trampling on their parents' "great expectations," even though, for the truly talented, this often amounts to cutting off the nose to spite the face. For this spite block finally to be lifted, an elaborate psychological reorientation toward the parents and toward oneself must take place, a therapeutic process that can consume years. The key event, of course, has nothing whatever to do with art; it involves a heroic act of emotional separation from the secret marriage to an intrusive parent that virtually every prodigy has internalized.

Sometimes such conflicts are resolved in the course of a lifetime, sometimes they are not. Often the resentment directed against a dominant parent stays in the unconscious and continues to be expressed in the form of a block; or, even if the person is actually able to write, she may be crippled by periodic bouts of self-destructiveness, such as episodes of alcoholism, the function of which is to keep her in a state of childlike dependence, saying to the parent, in effect, "You made me like this — now you can take care of me!" (At this point it is instructive for any reader who feels a sense of identification with these remarks to speak out loud the name of the person he has consecrated his life to spiting. No such problem gets resolved if it is not first formally acknowledged.)

Ex-prodigies, after years of suppressing a real inclination to art while obeying a stronger demand to grow up emotionally, may find their creative impulses reawakening in later life. If you are one of these people who find their resistance suddenly lifted after many years, you can return to writing confident that you are doing it for yourself. Your unconscious has judged you ready to begin again, to distill and shape what you have gained and lost from life.

It is even possible that the blocked prodigy who reenters the arena as that very different animal, a late bloomer, may enjoy the best of both worlds. He has had the early immersion in a discipline that leaves its unmistakable stamp; at the same time he has broken out of his womb-prison and had some contact with the world. If he has been able to acknowledge fully the loss of his childhood and replace it with other experiences, he can even take advantage of the ghostly presence of that intrusive parent, which, though it brings so many bad things, also cloaks the artist with a sense of invincibility that allows him to keep his self-confidence in the face of global rejection. For in the long run, as with all psychological burdens, perhaps the most pragmatic attitude we can take is: "I paid for this, in spades; now I'm going to get something out of it."

So if you are a young writer with a substantial oeuvre behind you and now, in spite of your earnest desires to continue, face a monumental block, that block is life. Accept it and enter without looking back. If the work is something that truly belongs to you, it will lead you back when you are ready. If it does not, better adventures await you — better because they were meant for you. No human is an island, and it is time to explore the archipelago.

THE ESCAPE FROM STRONG FEELINGS

The wish to seek shelter in the putative safety of the imagination when one needs to confront something directly in one's emotional life is not confined only to prodigies or ex-prodigies. In the face of tremendous emotional stress, this desire to flee into art can overwhelm any writer at any time. It can arise either because too much unresolved emotion is tied to the project at hand or because an accumulation of avoided problems hangs like a dark cloud over one's entire personal life.

But at the very moment the writer is desperately hoping to

jump into the hole of art and pull it in after her, the block rears up, impenetrable, barring the way. Here is Natalia Ginzburg:

> You cannot deceive yourself by hoping for caresses and lullabies from your vocation. In my life there have been interminable, desolate empty Sundays in which I desperately wanted to write something that would console me for my loneliness and boredom, so that I could be calmed and soothed by phrases and words. But I could not write a single line. My vocation has always rejected me, it does not want to know me. Because this vocation is never a consolation or a way of passing the time. It is not a companion.

Art does not allow itself to be used as a refuge from, or a substitute for, life; to try to make it that diminishes both the work and its creator.

But when you are in a state of great emotional distress or depression and your art refuses to know you, what are you to do to keep the writerly part of you alive without exploiting or falsifying it? When such an impasse occurs, some find it a relief to turn to expository writing or daily journal-keeping, since the delicate and complicated inner equilibrium that imaginative writing requires is impossible to maintain during these periods. Such is Ginzburg's theory:

> Our personal happiness or unhappiness, our *terrestrial* condition, has a great importance for the things we write.... When we are happy our imagination is stronger; when we are unhappy our memory works with greater vitality. Suffering makes the imagination weak and lazy; it moves, but unwillingly and heavily, with the weak movements of someone who is ill, with the weariness and caution of sick, feverish limbs; it is difficult for us to turn our eyes away from our own life and our own state, from the thirst and restlessness that pervade us.

At such times a diary can be a real lifesaver, as Kafka affirmed in his own daybook: "I must hold on here, it is the only place

I can." The daily act of translating reality into language, whether in a journal, diary, or the humble act of recording dreams, keeps the door open for a return to art.

Often, if you simply wait for the troubles to pass or the wound to heal, the block lifts of its own accord. But you must try to discriminate between justifiable hibernation and outright avoidance of deeper conflicts. Beware that the temporary turning away does not harden into permanent avoidance, either of the emotions or of the writing. Keep checking — keep knocking on the door — to see if you are ready to go back. Only by testing that is constant, gentle, and nonjudgmental will you be able to determine the state of your inner desires.

WITHDRAWAL OR ENGAGEMENT IS REFLECTED IN THE ART

Temporary withdrawal from the storms of life is not the same as permanent retreat, but the former condition has a sneaky habit of transforming itself into the latter. Many artists believe that if they only had a *lifelong* cabin in the woods, a place to live free from financial worries and somehow magically outside the concerns of daily life, they would be capable of much greater acts of art than they can perform in their current mundane setting.

I wonder. There is an old (and probably unreliable) story that the mystic philosopher Jakob Boehme, who had supported (barely) a wife and twelve children as a shoemaker, was finally granted a pension for life by his wealthy admirers, whereupon his visions promptly stopped. Rilke, plagued by writer's block, frequently fled his sculptress wife to find the perfect solitude in which to compose his verses free from untidy emotional obligations. To the dispassionate reader — more precisely, to the female reader — this kind of statement has the fishy smell of an excuse, not of a noble rationale. In fact, the prisoner of Duino Castle seems to have suffered just as mightily from his block away from home as in it. And would Kakfa have been able to render the ineffable grating of material reality against the fantastic with quite the same power if he had not been obliged, every day, to meet the world as a hard-working lawyer?

In truth, the boundary between art and life is not as clearly demarcated as we might like it to be. As Louise Bogan testifies, moral and emotional issues left unresolved in one realm often seep into the other.

> Poetry is an activity of the spirit; its roots lie deep in the subconscious nature, and it withers if that nature is denied, neglected, or negated. . . . A poet emerges from a spiritual crisis strengthened and refreshed only if he has been strong enough to fight it through at all levels, and at the deepest first. One refusal to take up the gage thrown down by his own nature leaves the artist confused and maimed. And it is not one confrontation, but many, which must be dealt with and resolved. The first evasion throws the poet back into a lesser state of development which no show of bravado can conceal. "A change of heart" is the result of slow and difficult inner adjustments. A mere shift in allegiance, if it not backed up by conflict genuinely resolved, produces in the artist, as it produces in anyone, confusion and insincerity.

Poets such as Rilke (she believes that he grew up) and Yeats, "because they fought their own battles on their own ground," Bogan says, "became, first, mature men, and then mature artists. They drew to themselves more and more experience; their work never dried up at the source or bloated into empty orotundity. The later poetry of both is work based on simple expression, deep insight, and deep joy."

Even when they do not produce a block, the artistic consequences of ducking these challenges can be dreadful. Evasiveness and withdrawal are always reflected, though in a curiously indirect way, in art. In a novelist's work, for example, they do not necessarily show up as evasive or withdrawn characters. It is far more likely that a writer retreating from specific emotional problems will create characters that are idealized *away from* the real source of malaise. When a wartime ambulance driver makes his main character a fearless soldier and killer of men, this subtle form of writerly dishonesty often goes completely unremarked by readers and critics. Withdrawal can also appear as lack of plot development or, more commonly, as a false resolution that conveniently sidesteps the real issues. Try as we will to disguise or avoid them, there is no escape from our shortcomings, either in the creative act or in its result. This process puts all our personal traits, positive and negative, through a sea change that fixes them as characteristic quirks of style, language, plot, character, vision — the personal traits, if you will, of a work of art.

Bogan's contemporary Robert Lowell, who knew whereof he spoke, also remarked on the devastating effects on their works when writers — in one of the hundreds of ways we all do, at different times in our lives, and sometimes without noticing the difference — mysteriously quit functioning as full human beings:

> When we examine Pope, Wordsworth, Coleridge, Arnold, or Browning, I think we realize that after a certain point all these men — all of them great writers at times and highly religious in their fashion — stopped living; they began to reflect, to imagine, to moralize: some single faculty kept on moving and fanning the air, but the whole-man had stopped. Consequently, in their writings they mused, they fabled, they preached, they schemed, and they damned.

Or, as Heinrich von Kleist said a few hundred years earlier, before taking his own life: "Ah, how bleak and empty and sad it must be to outlive one's heart."

LOGORRHEA: COMPULSIVE WRITING

Let's be brief: the world is overpopulated with words.
— STANISLAW JERZY LEC

Of all the "hiding from life" blocks, none is more striking, and more cleverly disguised as its opposite, than the phenomenon

of logorrhea, or compulsive writing. The extraordinarily prolific writer whose output flows unchecked is often an object of
awe for the blocked writer who, envying him in the same way
that an overweight person envies the anorexic, fails to see that
this deluge of words often conceals an inverted case of writer's
block. Like Hans Christian Andersen's little dancer who
couldn't get the enchanted red shoes off her feet, the compulsive writer cannot stop writing. Compulsive writing is, in fact,
a way of hiding from some of the deeper demands of literary
and emotional experience.

How can this be? Simply because for some writers, the act
of writing itself has taken on the aspect of a tic or other nervous
habit, meaningless except as a temporary relief and flight from
anxiety. These writers give birth to book after book not because their Muse of Realization is on 24-hour-a-day, 365-
day-a-year duty, but because they are in flight from their personal demons and writing provides the necessary fortification
within which to hide. Malcolm Lowry's biographer, Douglas
Day, indulging (perhaps too freely) in some literary psycho-
analysis, has speculated that

> ultimately, language — the emission of words — may come to
> be a defense against the dissolution of the personality. The
> death-wish, present in us all, is perhaps strongest in the oral
> type; who, having never really separated himself from the all-
> encompassing maternal elements, is in gravest danger of sub-
> siding back into it. If he is as acute as Malcolm Lowry was, he
> may recognize the lethal attraction of silence, and may write
> copiously, compulsively, in order not to die.

Whether or not denial of a death wish lies at the bottom of
compulsive writing, there is no doubt that it constitutes a defense of some sort, armor against unknown terrors, rather than
the constant unfolding expression of inner truth. This does
not mean that such writers never produce art, but merely that
a lot of what they do produce amounts to reflexive foot-tapping
in between their serious efforts.

To some extent, all humans try to duck the deeper strata of life, and for good reason: a great deal of it is very hard to bear. Writing itself, for writers, is a form of stress that we all try to avoid to the degree that we find it stressful. But whereas blocked writers tend to be those who discover their demons directly in the act of writing (and thus instinctively fear writing as an encounter with the unknown), compulsive writers experience (and try to avoid) that fearful confrontation in some other part of their psyches, causing them to flee *into* writing. In either case, the block involves keeping the production of verbiage (which by itself is no more than merely keeping the motor running) separate from a deeply felt artistic impulse. You cannot really claim you stay in constant high service of the Muse if you have to write the way other people have to smoke a cigarette.

Since overproduction is a less common form of writer's block than underproduction, it is harder to chart the progress of such writers. Do they occasionally become unable to write? Do they continue their awesome production to their dying day? Or am I merely writing out of the prejudices of modern times, overlooking such eras as the Victorian in England or the Golden Age of Spanish drama, when a voluminous output was standard operating procedure? (Anthony Trollope, dean of Victorian novelists, wrote fifty-four novels in addition to assorted travel books and belles lettres; Lope de Vega, the Spanish playwright of the sixteenth century cited by S. I. Witkiewicz's proud papa, wrote by his own estimate fifteen hundred plays.)

Overproducers have been a frequent target of scorn for many modern writers. In answer to the burning question "which is worse, to write too little or too much?" Cyril Connolly once stated:

> Sloth in writers is always a symptom of an acute inner conflict, especially that laziness which renders them incapable of doing the thing which they are most looking forward to, but their silence is better than . . . overproduction. . . . Slothful writers

such as Johnson, Coleridge, Greville, in spite of the nodding poppies of conversation, morphia, and horse-racing have more to their credit than Macaulay, Trollope or Scott.

Given the human propensity for seeking out "nodding poppies" — that is, mindless diversions — when one ought to be writing, Connolly is saying, in effect, that constipation is a condition more virtuous than diarrhea. At the least, such an opinion is a useful antidote to (if not an actual product of) the envy and despair a slow, erratic writer feels in comparing himself to the logorrheics. And Rilke, while plaintively admitting that

> I lacked that vitality of the great master [Rodin] which, little by little, had put him in a position to meet his inspiration unceasingly with so many work projects that it could not help acquiescing, almost without a pause coming up, to *one* of those offered,

still put his finger on the corresponding literary sin of the "steady" producers when he compared the principled silence of Tolstoy, who had given up his art for a cause, with the vast majority of writers who, with their regular and unremitting output, "were determined by practice and falsification (by 'literature') to conceal the occasional slackening or defection of their fruitfulness." The prolific writer is not necessarily more authentic and disciplined than the slow writer; she is likewise obeying the dictates of an instinctive (and uncontrollable) inner rhythm. Where it is a matter of art and not the manufacture of cars, more is not necessarily the same as better.

13
Success and Writer's Block

———— ❖ ————

"It's a blow upside the head," Claud said, smacking his temple. "Fame hits you like that. Even my dinky fame compared to a very large fame. It's like a comic strip. Whack! The guy's out cold, he sees stars, he's got this silly smile on his face. What it did, it was like I was forgiven for everything in my life which I shouldn't have done and for all those things I didn't do which I ought to have done, just because my past, my life, was exactly as it ought to have been, because if I hadn't lived such a life I wouldn't have got what I got, my dinky fame. It was proved to me that it's an all right world and God is an all right fellow. When I woke up, I wiped that smile off my face."
— GINA BERRIAULT
The Lights of Earth

WHAT IS commonly regarded as the best — success — I have saved for next to last. All writers are obliged first to define, and then to come to terms with, the presence or absence of this quantity in their careers. Personal standards of success, however, are inevitably influenced by the stereotypes that society hands down to us. Whether or not we measure up (or down) to these stereotypes constitutes the first identity crisis on the road to defining success in our own terms.

Literary success in Western industrial societies is often viewed simplistically as either "serious," with accompanying critical recognition, or "commercial," with mass readership and substantial financial reward taking the place of kudos. Both these types of success engender fame, the pinnacle of the success pyramid. American writers especially, because of what Saul Bellow has called this country's "major-league atmosphere in literature," tend to measure their own achievement in terms of the tiny handful who have achieved fame. But there are other, no less significant plateaus of outer-world success, ranging — in the most superficial terms — all the way from being published regularly to being published at all. And for the fortunate few with the inner fortitude to make this value genuinely their own and not just a rationalization, success means simply accomplishing what they set out to do in their work.

Most of us, unfortunately, have introjected the image of the Famous Writer of either category, serious or commercial, as a criterion of success. This standard inevitably becomes a powerful weapon against recalcitrant creativity: "Get busy this minute so I can be famous!" Such an undigested lump of ambition must be dealt with if we are to mature as writers and as persons. It cannot be repressed, the strategy of those who profess to care nothing about fame (don't believe them); nor can it be cravenly given in to, either by hero worship or by envy/hatred of the celebrated few. The desire for success is an impulse that can only be managed, not eradicated.

A pervasive and obsessive envy of others' success is usually the frog skin concealing the prince of unrealized potential. Envy allows us to duck the responsibility for our own uncultivated worth or talent and project these qualities onto others. The best antidote for envy is to convert it into fuel for real-world efforts to advance a career. Feeling envious takes energy. When that energy is rechanneled into perfecting the work and actively putting it forward, a negative emotion converts to a positive act of self-realization.

Understanding the mechanisms of fame is also useful in the process of coming to terms with the "success" shibboleth. By understanding, I do not mean sour grapes rationalizing that dismisses all famous writers as sellouts; such easy putdowns are often only one more disguised expression of envy. More to the point is understanding the underlying social, cultural, and especially economic forces that determine whether one writer and not another will become famous.

Literature is a commodity whose perceived value and contribution to culture varies enormously from society to society. In Pakistan, literature and its practitioners carry a much higher social status than they do in market-oriented Western technocracies. Audiences at readings recite poems along with the poet, hissing their appreciation at the end of favorite lines. Western Europe puts a different cultural value on literature than does Central or Eastern Europe. Latin American cultures differ from those in Asia. British Commonwealth countries such as Canada, New Zealand, and Australia have different expectations, in their desires to project a national identity via literature, than does Britain itself. The reception of a written work in a given cultural environment therefore always represents a relative, not an absolute, assessment of its worth. (There are no absolute assessments of literary worth.)

Far from being a discrete entity measurable by a single yardstick, literature as we know it amounts to a conglomeration of trends, fads, and biases, with proliferating schools and subschools. This is a difficult concept for writers within certain cultures to entertain. Most fiction writers in English-speaking countries, especially in the New World, find it strange to describe their work not simply in terms of content, but objectively in terms of type, style, and school. To *littérateurs* of other cultures, such ignorance of one's formal biases would be grotesque. North American prose writers, for example, tend to assume that realism is a kind of universal literary lingua franca instead of the recent highly stylized development it decidedly is. They are often equally blind to trends in world literature as well as in literary criticism, a field that, in cultures such as France, has a direct and immediate impact on literary styles. Yet not to know such basic facts about your literary identity and where it places you in a historical tradition means never to have the long-range perspective that allows a writer to make any kind of objective assessment about her literary fortunes.

Acquiring a bit of literary sophistication can give you something resembling a knowledgeable vantage point from which to view your work's reception in the world. For, apart from its literary merit — which you, its proud parent, will *never* be able to judge objectively — your work is going to be received within a specific cultural framework of unspoken literary assumptions determined by powerful social, intellectual, and economic biases. A multicultural and historical perspective, which so few writers trouble to acquire, will help you disengage with your work's critical reception (as discussed in Chapter 5). It can also make you skeptical of a success determined by chance trend and keep you cheerfully (well, almost cheerfully) unfazed by crushing failure.

A frivolous but illuminating way to uncover your present attitudes toward success and fame is to engage in an imaginary dialogue with the eminent writer, living or dead, whom you most admire. (To gain the full benefit of this experience, you must write it down on paper; that is the "making real" dimension of all writing exercises.) Because we frequently project our own not too well hidden lust for fame into a rivalry with such a person, you may be surprised at the twists, pleasant and unpleasant, this conversation can take — including the revelation of previously unsuspected values and attitudes you may hold on success and recognition.

With a few modest tools for framing the experience of success in hand, let's now turn to the severe blocks that its presence or absence can generate at various points in a writer's career.

FEAR OF SUCCESS

Oddly enough, fear of success is just as real an emotion — if rarely consciously acknowledged — in those who are far from achieving recognition as in those who are close to crossing the threshold. In fact, some writers remain obscure or unpublished because in some area of their souls they shrink from the expectation of what they imagine success will bring. As a rule, the block rises only when public recognition looms threateningly close on the horizon. Suppose you are a writer with only one more story to complete for a publisher to bring out your first collection. Stage fright, a kind of cosmic reluctance, seizes you and you find yourself unable to finish this story, or even begin it. Later, the contract canceled, you indulge in the "sweet lemon" rationalization that your artistic integrity kept you from cranking out a piece you didn't want to write just for the selfish pleasure of being published. Underneath, however, lurks the nagging, unconfronted truth: you did not want the book to be published. Why?

There are likely to be two possible answers, and it takes more honesty than anyone should reasonably be expected to have to determine which is right. The first is that you have sabotaged your chances out of an inner and unacknowledged sense of unworthiness — the demon of self-hatred at work again. But if you come to this bleak conclusion about your own motives, beware the temptation to create a closed circuit of self-blame in which you may now despise yourself for having spoiled your own chances.

A second reason for backing away from success is an unconscious conviction that you were not ready for national (or any public) exposure. Why weren't you ready? Again, many hypotheses may be worth considering. A lingering *puer* hesitation to cross the threshold into "actuality" may have affected you. Lack of publication, after all, represents a kind of incompletion or limitlessness; the products of your imagination become undeniably real when they are printed, bound, and placed in your hand. On the other hand, you may have been secretly convinced that your work, and possibly yourself as well, was not ready for the rollercoaster ride. Given the almost universal indifference that greets the vast majority of literary debuts, however, this fear of an impending flood of publicity is probably unwarranted.

If you are able to suspend punishing self-judgment and

consider any of the multitude of positive unconscious reasons you may have had for stumbling on the threshold of success, you are in an excellent position to rectify the situation. If it's shyness at the thought of any sort of public exposure, perhaps you require more practice in meeting the world in the company of your work by, for example, giving readings of your stories. Such experiences pave the way, in terms of emotional readiness, for accepting your own identity as a writer as well as for the appearance of a whole book. If your block arose from genuine doubts about the value of the work to be published, can you fix it? Or can you sit down now and write something better, something you will want the world to see? A gentle, nonblaming assessment is most likely to produce good results — instead of years of further paralysis and self-laceration. The missed opportunity, in fact, can be gained opportunity if you exploit it as an occasion to learn about your limitations and fears and work positively to grow through them.

Remember also that as a deliberate act performed by an experienced writer, refusal to publish either in mainstream venues or in "official" media can be a powerfully principled stand. This silence is most appropriate, of course, in the face of sanctions against free speech. But a writer can elect, as the poet Robert Duncan did, to spend many years shaping his most important work free from the potentially distorting influences of the literary environment. For the most part, this latter choice may be something only a literary nonvirgin is qualified to make: that is, you aren't really entitled to decide that public exposure and the influence of critics is no good for you unless you've actually had a taste of it first.

Under fear of success can also be subsumed fear of, or high-minded distaste for, the nuts and bolts of committing oneself to a literary career (as opposed to merely writing). Building a career is often mistaken for social climbing and manipulation. These elements of careerism exist as much in the literary field as any other; the only anomaly is that people don't like to believe it. I will never forget the gasp of incredulous horror that came from a classroom full of adults attending a writers' conference — all functioning professionals highly attuned to power jockeying in their own fields — when a witty poet dropped his public mask and let slip the fact that, among the notable poets who were to read that evening, there had been a certain amount of bad feeling about who was to go first — in public readings the least favorable slot. It was inconceivable to this audience of aspiring writers that *artistes* indulged in the same kind of ferocious in-house machinations as computer company executives or stockbrokers.

But power jockeying is not only pervasive in the literary world, it is also a powerful determinant in who gets the biggest piece of what is ultimately a rather small pie. The cold reality is that for all but a handful, fame is inextricably tied to worldliness and the ability to rise within a carefully demarcated hierarchy. There are two views on this phenomenon. The more conventional one can be found in the speech Honoré de Balzac put in the mouth of a minor character in his novel of a young writer's progress, *Lost Illusions.* Seizing the young provincial poet Lucien by the lapels, this denizen of the literary demimonde exclaims pitifully:

> My poor young poet, I came to Paris, like you, full of illusions, impelled by the love of art, and by an unconquerable desire for glory. . . . My lofty ideals — which I now have well under control — my first youthful enthusiasm — prevented me from seeing the workings of the social machinery; I was compelled to see it in the end by bumping against its wheels, knocking into its shafts, getting covered with its grease, and hearing the constant clatter of its chains and fly-wheels. . . . Outside the literary world . . . there is no one who has the slightest idea of the terrible Odyssey by which writers reach what is called vogue, or fashion, or reputation, fame, celebrity, public favour. . . . This fine thing reputation that is so much desired is nearly always crowned prostitution.

The irony here is that while Lucien eventually returns, disillusioned, to the provinces, his creator Balzac was positioned squarely at the top of the literary pyramid even as he wrote these lines. With this consideration in mind, we can turn to the other side of this debate, made by the poet Stephen Spender to defend William Butler Yeats (and coincidentally himself) against the charge of literary politicking and logrolling, activities that Yeats's diaries revealed him to be very much engaged in. Arguing that it was Yeats's "Dublin intrigues and squabbles out of which he made poems harder and clearer than his early 'twilight' poetry," Spender uses the same imagery that Balzac did to make the opposite point:

> The dyer's hand is not just stained with the dye of his trade and occupation, it is also, when it is making the cloth of his poetry, stained with the grease, oil, and much of the world that surrounds him, the society in which he moves. In his later work Yeats, who had been a minor poet in his youth, transformed the world in which he lived, of politics, theater, business, and sex, into poetry.

Whether one is anointed by or drowned in the axle grease of literary careerism seems to be, as usual, a strictly individual matter, though there are perhaps more examples of its detrimental effects than of its positive influence on creativity.

Yet whether it is done out of a sense of high-mindedness or shyness, a writer's resistance to participate in the literary community can materially block or delay the publication of his work. As a writer you must be willing to put yourself forward, again and again; this is not narcissism but simple survival. If you have a deep-seated resistance to doing this, you must be willing to ask yourself honestly whether you are showing a greater dedication to your art or, out of an insidious lack of self-confidence, you do not believe in your heart that you belong in the company of writers.

But what happens to the writer who finally does arrive, late or early, at the end of that "terrible Odyssey" to fame? Let's turn to the role that inner resistance plays at this juncture in a writer's lifetime.

ACHIEVING SUCCESS

Whom the gods would destroy, they first call promising.
— CYRIL CONNOLLY

Success offers expanded opportunities and equally expanded pitfalls. It provides a wider audience and sometimes financial rewards that allow more time to write, along with a gratifying endorsement of the years of solitary effort it took the writer to get this far. Success imparts that incomparable feeling of flowing with the current after years of ceaseless struggle upstream against indifference and rejection. And the impetus and validation that success provides can spur a writer to much greater efforts than she might otherwise have attempted.

But success can also bring trouble when a writer identifies with fame instead of finding his own center. A large and sudden success — which happens more frequently in the arts than in other professions, where the transition is usually far more gradual and predictable — can leave a writer open to stage fright at the prospect of letting down a much larger audience, or to the harsh and often envious criticism from others that comes with being a visible target. Writers who have this experience find themselves at the mercy of a childlike inflation they never even knew they possessed. Megalomania, complete panic, or both rear their strange and frightening heads.

A writer who has become not merely successful but famous may succumb to the temptation of making fame itself a new career, with writing a secondary concern. In North America especially, literary achievement tends to be confused with celebrity status and personal charisma. In *The Frenzy of Renown*, Leo Braudy has pointed out that fame in the United States is antihistorical, a kind of secularized sainthood, and this greater isolation of individuals from a tradition leaves American celebrities far more vulnerable than, say, their European counterparts. Fame on these terms, the *People* magazine variety, is based on a cult of personality that needs to create easily recognizable star personae. "The exemplary famous person here is especially the person famous for being himself or playing himself," Braudy says. "The less you actually had to do or create in order to be famous, the more truly famous you are for yourself, your spirit, your soul, your inner nature."

This kind of fame represents the ultimate self-fulfillment and self-punishment of narcissism because it crystallizes — and traps — an image of the writer as a personality who supplants his own works as the primary focus of interest. James Baldwin once told an interviewer:

> One of the hazards of being an American writer, and I'm well placed to know it, is that eventually you have nothing to write about. . . . There is a decidedly grave danger of becoming a celebrity, of becoming a star, of becoming a personality. . . . It's symptomatic of the society that doesn't have any real respect for the artist. You're either a success or a failure and there's nothing in between. And if you are a success, you run the risk of becoming a kind of show business personality. Then the legend becomes far more important than the work. It's as though you're living in an echo chamber. You hear only your own voice. And, when you become a celebrity, that voice is magnified by multitudes and you begin to drown in this endless duplication of what looks like yourself. . . . The moment you carry the persona to the typewriter, you are finished.

Many writers, isolated by their success and unsupported by a strong intellectual or cultural tradition, have found themselves unable to bring anything *but* their persona to the typewriter, and this is the moment when silence falls.

For one thing, the newly successful writer's inability to perform may signify an unconscious revolt against the expectations of a voracious public. The word "fame" derives from the Latin *fama*, meaning rumor or ill report — as if fame inevitably carries with it the collective worship and resentment of a whole society. In this context the block performs possibly the same symbolic function for writers as the weight problem of certain movie stars who, one suspects, get fat as an unconscious but heartfelt rebellion against the burden of the sexual projections of millions of other humans.

To make matters worse, success has a distressingly random quality that makes it especially hard for the individual writer to come to terms with. As Braudy put it: "From the log cabin to the White House, from the chorus to center stage, the myth said that the indomitable natural talent drew the spotlight to itself. Yet in darker moments it was also clear that the spotlight moved by its own compulsions and for its own reasons."

As a writer you can never know for sure whether the rewards of success are deserved or undeserved, except as they resonate with your own sense of what is right. If what Rilke called the inner conscience has been twisted beyond recognition between the twin poles of inferiority and inflation, you will be the public's puppet, relying on them to tell you what's right or wrong with your work instead of making a balanced judgment yourself. And the minute you hand over your creative tiller to the world at large, you are likely to experience a tremendous block. You have become partners with your public instead of with that hidden side of you, which doesn't like the new state of affairs one bit.

Moreover, success gained primarily by manipulation of the literary environment carries no inner validation and may leave its recipient not just smeared with axle grease but drowned in it. This is especially the case of truly gifted young writers who have also shown a precocious but ultimately fatal ability to maneuver themselves into the "right place at the right time." They find themselves acclaimed for the works they wrote in decent obscurity, but now — in the full glare of publicity, with an enormous advance in the bank for the next work — the essential fraudulence of the rapid rise they or others engineered is likely to overwhelm them.

Other writers discover a new equilibrium in the specialized world of bestsellerdom; once in the limelight they have no difficulty adapting their talent to the situation at hand. It is precisely that overambitious person with a genuine, strange, noncommercial talent who is most likely to be done in. Such a young person discovers that he has hoisted himself into a place he is neither emotionally nor artistically up to handling, and never recovers from being kicked, or kicking himself, upstairs. Impelled, for example, by the dream of becoming a Great Poet, he discovers that his finest creation has been a Great Career, and there is nothing, absolutely nothing but technique, lying at the center of it.

This sense of fraudulence is not confined to the writer himself. The growing self-estrangement such a writer feels may also eventually, even beneath the hype of the Famous Author, be detected by readers. "The advertising, publicity and enthusiasm which a book generates — in a word its success — imply a reaction against it," Cyril Connolly noted. "The element of inflation in a writer's success, the extent to which it has been forced, is something that has to be written off. One can fool the public about a book but the public will store up resentment in proportion to its folly." He adds ominously, "The public can be fooled deliberately, by advertising and publicity, or it can be fooled by accident, by the writer fooling himself." The emergence of a block is the sign that the writer has, on an unconscious level, stopped fooling himself.

Success and fame, especially when it comes too soon, can thus effectively stunt a writer's further development. Dylan Thomas's notebooks reveal the startling information that this poet's major creative output occurred between the ages of fifteen and nineteen, a time when he wrote the drafts of most of his major works; comparable new creative activity did not occur during the alcohol-soaked term of his meteoric fame before his death at age thirty-nine. As with all the others who didn't have a chance to grow up in private, the arc of Thomas's career followed the prodigy's pattern. John Raeburn's study of Hemingway, *Fame Became of Him*, makes a fitting epitaph to this tragic group.

It is the young writer who runs the highest risk of having produced an outstanding work — like the boy's airplane fuselage in Chapter 5, an interesting fluke — that, in the words of science, "cannot be replicated." To compose that one perfect autobiographical novel, this writer may have emptied a very small bank account of everything it held in the way of life experience and art, and another ten years may need to pass for equivalent reserves to reaccumulate. If you are that person, do you have the fortitude it takes to retreat from the public gaze and let your life savings grow back in private?

Writers who become well known only later in life and who avoid superstar status find it easier to make the transition to the special demands of wide public recognition. But even experienced writers can be stricken with the too-much-free-time malaise; the eternal youth can resurface in a serious producing writer who, after years of scrambling to make ends meet, becomes financially secure from writing. This new freedom can have the effect of making its recipient feel as shiftless as a teenager, creating an atmosphere of paralysis and collapsing a long-standing writing routine after the "petty" demands of earning a daily living are removed.

Many writers find themselves completely blocked by this removal of mundane pressures, the anticipated heaven turning out to be hell instead. It is as if you had been granted lifetime tenure at an opulent writers' colony and began slowly to realize that you didn't much relish the prospect. You experience the dread limitlessness of having all the time in the world to write, fertile breeding ground for guilt when your unconscious is in full-scale rebellion against the "successful" and "serious" labels. In just this condition of external plenty and internal famine John Steinbeck, famous at last, lamented: "The perfect pointed pencil — the paper persuasive — the fantastic chair and a good light and no writing."

Writing, as Hemingway once admitted, is not a full-time occupation. You have to do something with the rest of that time, and this is where the marlin fishing — or worse — begins. As a rule, such paralysis doesn't strike either the confirmed "pros," those who write formulaic genre books, or the serious writers who have formed a solid sense of themselves and their works, but rather the sensitive writers who might, if they were not already so well known for writing a certain way, have the courage to strike out on a new adventure in art that could take them years and many false starts to complete.

Many books do manage to get written out of the spiritual limbo that comes with this complicated adjustment to success, but, as we saw in Chapter 10, they are often lifeless works, produced by forcing the block just because the writer feels that, as a Famous Author, she *ought* to be writing even if her inner creative mechanisms have not wholly adapted to the frightening new environment of success.

For all but the most strong-minded, then, success can be an unexpectedly challenging experience. Finding one's center again after being swept into the maelstrom is no easy thing to do. A writer who finds herself in any version of this dilemma can take a few small, practical steps backward to defuse the highly charged situation. She can, for example, refuse to accept any portion of the huge new advance until the manuscript is finished or at least safely begun; in this way, she has given herself the freedom and time to engage in all the false starts necessary before something genuine emerges. She can continue as much as possible her old way of life and her old way of earning a living to avoid a radical departure from routine. All the time she must be seeking, actively seeking, that small quiet place way to the left of the limelight in which to carry on her real life of the heart, because it is in that humble spot exactly, not media center stage, that her next work will take shape.

NOT ACHIEVING SUCCESS

What of the other and far more common side of the success coin? What of the writer who has struggled for years and years with only modest returns for his efforts? What if he has never been allowed to experience that marvelous feeling of being buoyed by public esteem? Such a writer feels helpless and frustrated; the nagging voice inside, in perfect harmony with the superficial standards of his society, tells him that the public's indifference to him — as to any number of worthless writers — is deadly accurate: You deserve to be unknown because you're no good.

Since success is so often measured in chintzy and antiliterary terms, it is not just essential but lifesaving for each writer to formulate an individual standard of success more in keeping with reality — his own as opposed to that of the world around him. Nevertheless, raw and unjust neglect carries its own intrusive reality that cannot be rationalized away. Lack of success can have highly detrimental effects on a writer's work, and the moral gymnastics required to "rise above" indifference can be exhausting when they are performed over a lifetime.

So many gifted persons have suffered undeservedly that popular wisdom tends to be a bit blasé about this circumstance, declaring that it is the "artist's lot." For the serious writer, however, lack of recognition is an unnatural state of affairs that benefits neither the writer nor her potential public. Randall Jarrell had this to say about the career of the novelist Christina Stead after the critical failure of her magnificent *The Man Who Loved Children:*

> When the world rejects, and then forgets, a writer's most profound and imaginative book, he may unconsciously work in a more limited way in the books that follow it; this has happened, I believe, to Christina Stead. The world's incomprehension has robbed it, for twenty-five years, of *The Man Who Loved Children;* has robbed it, forever, of what could have come after *The Man Who Loved Children.*

The failure to achieve deserved success — critical recognition or even publication — can cause an actual block as well as a subtle diminishment of effort. Such a writer thinks: Why sit down and write yet another novel/story/poem to be sent out fifty times with no results? Why bring it into the world at all if no one wants to read it? These are gut feelings that deserve to be taken seriously — though always with the caveat that the "no one" out there is not the whole world but an overselected handful of literary arbiters. Your decision to continue as a writer must be, as always, an individual one. Some experience relief in laying down their pens after years of frustration; others do not.

The writer who soldiers on in spite of everything has probably experienced an inner decision that has consciously or unconsciously adapted him, or resigned him, to an "invisible" identity. His obscurity may be warranted or it may not, but he continues to function as a writer just the same. What often gets forgotten is that the vast majority of writers live out their literary lives in just such a penumbra. Only a handful stand in the sun — if that is really the right image — and even these few have usually put in a twenty-year apprenticeship in the shadows.

Once again, the benefits of an environment of benign neglect on literary endeavor cannot be overemphasized. Taken in the proper spirit — and this requires careful conscious discrimination, not defensive rationalizing — indifference is liberating. Over the long haul it exerts a healthy influence on your work, certainly far healthier than the glare of publicity and the review machinery of national publications. Most writers experience an extremely long formative period (if not their entire creative lifetimes) during which they remain highly suggestible to outside influence. As an unknown, you are free to develop and strengthen your creative identity during this important time; the tentative whisper of your unconscious, with whom you are developing your primary literary relationship, is not being drowned out by the loud, authoritarian voice of critical opinion. Conversely, if obscurity descends on you again after an initial flurry of recognition, you have the rare opportunity to understand just how fickle and irrational the climate of critical opinion can be. It is an opportunity that allows you to *become exactly what you are,* an opportunity those riding the crest of trend and fashion never get. Overidentified with public opinion, they are likely to become its prisoners instead.

This is not to belittle those obvious talents who succeed,

and deservedly, regardless of the current fashion. But even favored writers often end up having their wrists slapped for failure to conform to the prevailing literary sensibility. Here only the strength of the inner attitude the writer has cultivated through good times and bad will save her from total despair. Writers such as Jean Rhys, for example, not "discovered" until old age when their actual writing careers were virtually over, may often sound bitter on the surface, but underneath lies the luminous core of understanding that has sustained them: "All of writing is a huge lake. There are great rivers that feed the lake, like Tolstoy and Dostoyevsky. And there are trickles, like Jean Rhys. All that matters is feeding the lake. I don't matter. The lake matters. You must keep feeding the lake."

Rhys's attitude vividly illustrates the differences between what might be called the ensemble or repertory view of literature — equally supportive of lead, second-string, and bit players — and the star system, which eats its prey alive. The ensemble ethic supports not just the individual writer but the tradition she carries as well. We, as writers, are bearers of a culture, a language, and a tradition — a fact we often brush aside in our egotistical quest for personal acclaim.

For just this reason I have deliberately avoided a roll call of great writers who were neglected for much of their lifetimes. What has Melville's example, or any one of a hundred such stories, to do with most writers? There is no such thing as a model literary career, either for success or for obscurity. Untold great writers have stayed neglected and unknown, their books out of print, their manuscripts lost. It is a fallacy to believe that some Cosmic Rehabilitator causes all the deserving to be lifted out of obscurity after their deaths and restored to their rightful places in the pantheon of art. Only a few scholars, generation after generation, trouble to do this, and we do not always bother to listen to them.

Moreover, none of us is a Melville or a van Gogh, or a Thomas Mann or a Goethe, for that matter; each of us has an individual destiny as a person and as a writer. To keep the conundrum of success in perspective, it helps to ask this question: Is the success of the art more important than, on one hand, simply having accomplished it as well as one can, and, on the other, the success of the life itself? For whether your books are out of print or bestsellers, they won't be the ones — as the saying goes — who cry at your wake.

I 4
Active Silence

———— ❖ ————

Who then . . . tells a finer tale than any of us? Silence does.
—ISAK DINESEN

ALL KINDS of silences, unscheduled and unexplained, are likely to fall in every writer's life. This book has examined some involuntary silences geared to fend off the unreasonable demands of a psyche in disequilibrium and has suggested ways of lifting these silences. But silence is not a condition that demands rectification every time. Even for a writer, silence is not always, or even mostly, a bad thing.

Silence is often as blessed a condition as its opposite. Writing/not writing represents a natural alternation of states, an instinctive rhythm that lies at the heart of the creative process. To steal a metaphor from Coleridge (who stole it from the Germans), they are the inseparable systole and diastole, the contraction and expansion, of the creative experience. This rhythm, moreover, takes a unique shape from artist to artist. For every writer who is a relentlessly systematic worker, another is not. For every writer who allows a month of silence to fall between works, another allows a year.

Some silences in a writing life may be blameworthy (that is, to fall silent when it is one's moral duty to speak up), but most are likely to be not merely "acts of God" but central experiences of the creative life — the negative space that surrounds and supports every act of art. The silence merely *is;* only the writer errs in refusing its right to existence. Besides the stifled silence resulting from censorship and oppression, then, many kinds of natural internal silences happen to writers: thwarted unhappy silences; beautiful, restful silences; the deep silence of emotional grief; the fertile silence of creative incubation. Let's examine a few of these active silences.

THE SILENCE OF INCUBATION

For many writers, including those who would not otherwise describe themselves as blocked, the gulf that yawns between intent and execution remains a highly mysterious and unpredictable event. Few would fail to recognize the state Jean Cocteau described when he lamented that it never seemed possible to "do what one *intends*":

> I feel myself inhabited by a force or being — very little known to me. It gives the orders; I follow. The conception of my novel *Les Enfants Terribles* came to me from a friend. . . . I commenced to write: exactly seventeen pages per day. It went well. I was pleased with it. Very. There was in the original life story some connection with America, and I had something I wanted to say about America. Poof! The being in me did not want to write that! Dead halt. A month of stupid staring at paper unable to say anything. One day it commenced again in its own way. . . .
>
> When you speak of these things to one who works systematically . . . they think you jest. Or that you are lazy and use this as an excuse. Put yourself at a desk and write! You are a writer, are you not? *Voilà!* I have tried this. What comes is no good. *Never any good.* Claudel at his desk from nine to twelve. It is unthinkable to work like that!

Cocteau is describing the active internal state Keats called "delicious diligent indolence," the silence that falls in the house of art while an idea is developing out of sight, down in the basement.

This is exactly the kind of unpredictable, irrational silence that overly controlling writers find unendurable. Such writers are unlikely to have Cocteau's blithe reaction, a Gallic shrug of the shoulders over his inability to keep either his writing schedule or the narrative on its preconceived track. The controlling personality thinks: "That story about 'letting the field lie fallow' is the world's hoariest excuse for laziness. Nothing's happening down there — I know because *I* don't feel anything happening. I'm just stalling again."

We know already that "laziness" and "stalling" are the buzzwords of an autocratic, punishing consciousness. That consciousness is unaware that anything is happening because the unconscious is shielding its sprouting seeds from the prematurely judgmental ego. Consciousness will not be allowed in the garden until the plants are tall enough and tough enough to withstand its hobnailed boots. Then, and only then, will it be granted entry.

If you belong to this category of impatient writers, it is vital that you consciously adopt a positive, accepting attitude toward your silences both before and during a writing project. Patience, acceptance, and trust are the virtues your consciousness must cultivate while the unconscious is active. Rollo May has given a precise description of this state of conscious inactivity coupled with unconscious activity:

> An artist's "waiting," funny as it may look in cartoons, is not to be confused with laziness or passivity. It requires a high degree of attention, as when a diver is poised on the end of the springboard, not jumping but holding his or her muscles in sensitive balance for the right second. It is an active listening, keyed to hear the answer, alert to see whatever can be glimpsed when the vision or the words do come. It is a waiting for the birthing process to begin to move in its own organic time. It is necessary that the artist have this sense of timing, that he or she respect these periods of receptivity as part of the mystery of creativity and creation.

The more a writer persists in developing her skills of active waiting, the stronger the bond of trust becomes between the conscious ego and that mysterious entity on the other side. As an added benefit, the intervals of silence may even decrease in proportion to the writer's unquestioning respect for them.

THE SILENCE OF GRIEF

Another silence that commands obedience is the silence of emotional grief as it works through to resolution in the deeper strata of your psyche. Whereas some find the act of writing itself a cathartic release after a scarcely bearable life episode — and others, in addition, have produced great works of art in the *recollection* of grief — a sizable number of writers find this door barred to them and retreat into silence.

Though the circumstances may be tragic, such a silence is also positive. Mourning is an active condition, not to be confused with the attempt to escape from feelings discussed in Chapter 12. At such times, the full energies of the unconscious may be taken up in the knitting and healing process, leaving nothing left over for creative endeavor. Surrendering oneself to this unseen, sometimes even unfelt, process requires the blind faith that progress is somehow being made. When the heart cries, "I don't *want* to write," the head must be willing to listen and heed. "You have to realize," Natalia Ginzburg said, "that you cannot hope to console yourself for your grief by your writing."

A case of a writer who tried and failed to find direct release from intolerable grief through his work is that of Stéphane Mallarmé, who planned a literary memorial to his son Anatole, dead at the age of eight. The notes he left for this ambitious work, never finished, reveal a desperate intention to cheat death of its victory by the time-honored device of immortalizing the deceased through art. Yet as the critic Leo Bersani commented, "Mallarmé's failure to complete the Anatole epic is perhaps the sign of a reluctance to reduce life to the trivializing nobility of redemption through art." When Ben Jonson lost a son of the same age, the epitaph he composed put the emphasis in its proper place: "Rest in soft peace, and, ask'd, say here doth lye/Ben Jonson his best piece of poetrie."

Grief can certainly be expressed and to a degree resolved through writing, but being consistently successful at doing so uncovers a certain cannibalistic tendency, the dark side of a writer's incorporation of her life into her art. In *Child's Play* the Australian novelist David Malouf paints an ironic portrait of a fictitious "great man of letters" for whom every detail in the lives of his intimates, every tragedy including the accidental death of his son, seems to serve solely as grist for his creative mill. When this writer devotes himself with his usual inexorable self-discipline to composing a memorial letter to his son, "there was no doubting the old man's grief," the narrator comments, "but somehow one is embarrassed by the surge of renewed energy that comes to him with this new stroke of fate, the opportunity it offers to show once again his powers of mastery. *The work, the Work*. Everything in the end becomes simply another proof of his extraordinary genius, his capacity to turn life's bitter hardships into the stuff of art."

This is a familiar, if awful, narcissism, one every writer recognizes. Viewed in this light, Mallarmé's block may have represented as well the victory of his own humanity over an artist's monolithic self-absorption.

Art is not superior to life. Works of art are not sacred idols defying time and space; they are artifacts and playful representations of the human spirit that lack those magical redemptive powers which we might want to grant them. If we try to exploit art as a means of canceling out or even capitalizing on the real losses life imposes on us, the shallow need that motivates this act will diminish both the life and the art.

THE SILENCE OF THREE POEMS A YEAR

Philip Larkin, calculating his creative output of a lifetime for an interviewer, reckoned that it worked out on average to three poems a year. In his and other such cases, that negative space around the three poems per year looms large in retrospect. Blaming oneself for low productivity, however — an activity Larkin himself engaged in only in private — is punishment for a crime that did not exist until it was named. An uneven artistic output, for many, is a natural condition of creativity.

There is also, for example, our favorite whipping boy Coleridge, author of "Rime of the Ancient Mariner" on one hand and scores of unfulfilled outlines, plans, and proposals on the other. Earlier I quoted Cyril Connolly praising Coleridge's silence, and here is E. M. Forster's matching epitaph:

> He seldom did what he or what others hoped, and posterity has marked him as her prey in consequence. She had never ceased to hold up her plump finger to him, and shake it and say that he has disappointed her. . . . But if one turns on posterity and says, "Well! what else do you want him to do? Would you rather have [Coleridge] as he is or not at all?" she is apt to be silent or to change the conversation.

As with Connolly, more than disinterested championing of an author may have been at work here, as Forster's own fictional output was relatively small, a fact that prompted Elizabeth Bowen to comment: "Mr. Forster's intervals of silence have been a perplexity, as well as a deprivation. Silences, in a man from whom we have exorbitant expectations, take on a sort of positive character."

In this way, perversely, with the collective anticipation of their audience bestowing special intensity on their few works, the extended silences of such writers end up carrying tremendous resonance.

RANDOM SILENCES

Again and again the invisibility, the inaccessibility, of unconscious processes tempts us as writers to worry whenever silence falls. We do not ask it to fall; it does so entirely on its own. Because the conscious self receives no messages, it assumes that nothing is happening. Sometimes this may be the case, but not always. A great deal of self-confidence is required to distinguish an active, incubating silence from just plain silence. And a writer must be able to call the judgment every time.

When you as a writer find yourself in the middle of a silence, consider above all treating it with dignity. Resist your first impulse to squash it like a bug; you are likely to fail in this attempt, in any event. Examine your relationship to your work in all the areas described in earlier chapters. If none of them seems to be the motive, you must still be prepared to accept and acknowledge your "block" as an unidentifiable active silence. Give the unconscious some credit. You may never know exactly why it has drawn back from you, but you must respect its need to do so. For the time being, you must concede the fact that it is not in your control; you are in its control. The less you resist your resistance, the more alert you are likely to be to the moment it is ready to change into something else.

A seemingly gratuitous silence imposed on the ego is part of the inherent irrationality of life. It is galling, after all, that we are never smart enough, clear sighted enough, or prescient enough to see the full scope of our lives or art, or their future direction, at any given moment. Artists especially, concerned as they are with shaping and forming, can find this a hard pill to swallow. Even those artists who reject the idea of "meaning" are reluctant to accept that the source and continuity of their work are rooted in something entirely outside their conscious control.

As writers we do not want to accept that our life in art is not, and will never be, a steady linear progression into the sunlight — that it is actually a series of advances and retreats, stops and starts, unfoldings and closings up. We do not want to accept that our powers will be working inside us more strongly at some times than at others, with the result that some of our works will be markedly better than others — and not necessarily in chronological sequence. We do not want to accept that we have control over only certain areas of our art and not all of it. But we must. And it is not at all a bad thing that we are obliged to do so.

THE·LAST WORD

The day a person finds out he's a writer is usually not the day he finishes his first story or poem or the day he is first published, but much, much farther down the road. It is the day he realizes he possesses a certain cluster of psychological traits that forms the writing obsession. Far from feeling crowned with laurel, this person is likely to experience a reaction akin to hearing, on his twenty-first birthday, that he is descended from a venerable line of Transylvanian vampires and he is one, too; there is no escape! For by this time he has probably had ample opportunity to observe, in himself and in other writers, some of the psychological stigmata of the creative person: hypersensitivity, self-absorption, compulsive behavior, ungenerous ambition, and all those related traits that tend to cancel out the romantic aura the profession holds in the eyes of the uninitiated.

There is another side to this depressing realization, and that is a simple distinction between neurosis and art. It is not neurotic to sit at a desk all day devising an imaginary world. It is not even neurotic to sit all day at a desk trying to devise an imaginary world but not succeeding in doing so. What *is* neurotic is to hate oneself for doing or not doing either of these activities. Let Otto Rank speak to the point:

> The neurotic, no matter whether productive or obstructed, suffers fundamentally from the fact that he cannot or will not accept himself, his own individuality, his own personality. On one hand he criticizes himself to excess, which means that he makes too great demands on himself and his completeness, so that failing to attain leads only to more self-criticism. If we take this thwarted type . . . and compare him to the artist, it is at

once clear that the artist is in a sense the antithesis to the self-critical neurotic type. Not that the artist does not criticize himself, but by accepting his personality he not only fulfills that for which the neurotic is striving in vain but goes far beyond it. The precondition, then, of the creative personality is not only its acceptance but its actual glorification of itself.

Viewed in Rank's benign perspective, the frissons of egotism and other eccentricities often found in the creative personality are, like a mild dose of asbestos poisoning, to be taken merely as occupational hazards — nothing terminal.

For our purposes, however, Rank has identified the most important silence available to the creative person — namely, the active verb "to silence." For a writer, this must be truly the last word. In silencing the voice of relentless self-hatred, the writer gains in fulfilled humanity as well as art. That triumphant silencing, when it is renewed daily, has consequences that echo for a lifetime.

Appendix

———— ❖ ————

THE PERSON FROM PORLOCK: A PORTFOLIO

When the poem "Kubla Khan" was published in 1816, Samuel Taylor Coleridge appended the following explanation of its fragmentary nature. The statement's suspect plausibility has created a lingering ripple in English literary history, as suggested by the two poetical responses by the twentieth-century poets Robert Graves and Stevie Smith.*

In the summer of the year 1797, the Author, then in ill health, had retired to a lonely farm-house between Porlock and Linton, on the Exmoor confines of Somerset and Devonshire. In consequence of a slight indisposition, an anodyne had been prescribed, from the effects of which he fell asleep in his chair at the moment that he was reading the following sentence, or words of the same substance, in "Purchas's Pilgrimage": "Here the Khan Kubla commanded a palace to be built, and a stately garden thereunto. And thus ten miles of fertile ground were inclosed with a wall." The Author continued for about

* Vladimir Nabokov's working title for his novel *Bend Sinister* was "Person from Porlock." In this choice, Nabokov aficionados will recognize the master's delight in weaving authorial self-consciousness into the fabric of his art.

three hours in a profound sleep, at least of the external senses, during which time he had the most vivid confidence, that he could not have composed less than from two to three hundred lines; if that indeed can be called composition in which all the images rose up before him as *things,* with a parallel production of the correspondent expressions, without any sensation or consciousness of effort. On awaking he appeared to himself to have a distinct recollection of the whole, and taking his pen, ink, and paper, instantly and eagerly wrote down the lines that are here preserved. At this moment he was unfortunately called out by a person on business from Porlock, and detained by him above an hour, and on his return to his room, found, to his no small surprise and mortification, that though he still retained some vague and dim recollection of the general purport of the vision, yet, with the exception of some eight or ten scattered lines and images, all the rest had passed away like the images on the surface of a stream into which a stone has been cast, but, alas! without the after restoration of the latter!

The Person from Porlock

Unkind fate sent the Porlock person
To collect fivepence from a poet's house;
Pocketing which old debt he drove away,
Heedless and gay, homeward bound for Porlock.

O Porlock person, habitual scapegoat,
Should any masterpiece be marred or scotched,
I wish your burly fist on the front door
Had banged yet oftener in literature!

— ROBERT GRAVES

Thoughts About the Person from Porlock

Coleridge received the Person from Porlock
And ever after called him a curse,
Then why did he hurry to let him in?
He could have hid in the house.

It was not right of Coleridge in fact it was wrong
(But often we all do wrong)
As the truth is I think he was already stuck
With Kubla Khan.

He was weeping and wailing: I am finished, finished,
I shall never write another word of it,
When along comes the Person from Porlock
And takes the blame for it.

It was not right, it was wrong,
But often we all do wrong.

May we inquire the name of the Person from Porlock?
Why, Porson, didn't you know?
He lived at the bottom of Porlock Hill
So had a long way to go,

He wasn't much in the social sense
Though his grandmother was a Warlock,
One of the Rutlandshire ones I fancy
And nothing to do with Porlock,

And he lived at the bottom of the hill as I said
And had a cat named Flo,
And had a cat named Flo.

I long for the Person from Porlock
To bring my thoughts to an end,
I am becoming impatient to see him
I think of him as a friend,

Often I look out of the window
Often I run to the gate
I think, He will come this evening,
I think it is rather late.

I am hungry to be interrupted
For ever and ever amen
O Person from Porlock come quickly
And bring my thoughts to an end.

I felicitate the people who have a Person from Porlock
To break up everything and throw it away

Because then there will be nothing to keep them
And they need not stay.

Why do they grumble so much?
He comes like a benison
They should be glad he has not forgotten them
They might have had to go on.

These thoughts are depressing I know. They are depressing,
I wish I was more cheerful, it is more pleasant,
Also it is a duty, we should smile as well as submitting
To the purpose of One Above who is experimenting
With various mixtures of human character which goes best
All is interesting for him it is exciting, but not for us.
There I go again. Smile, smile, and get some work to do
Then you will be practically unconscious without positively
    having to go.

— STEVIE SMITH

Notes

———— ❖ ————

Frontispiece quote from *The Diaries of Franz Kafka 1910–1913*, ed. Max Brod (New York: Schocken Books, 1965), p. 264.

page   PREFACE

xi Heinrich von Kleist, "On the Gradual Formation of Ideas in Speech," from *An Abyss Deep Enough*, ed. and trans. Philip B. Miller (New York: E. P. Dutton, 1982), p. 222.

CHAPTER I

1 Jean Cocteau, interview, *Writers at Work: The Paris Review Interviews*, 3rd series, ed. George Plimpton (New York: Penguin Books, 1978), p. 67.

1 Tillie Olsen, *Silences* (New York: Delacorte Press/Seymour Lawrence, 1978), p. 6; George Eliot, *Middlemarch* (New York: Harcourt, Brace and World, 1962), p. 275. For a discussion of the origin of the term "writer's block" in the twentieth-century psychoanalytic movement, see Zachary Leader, *Writer's Block* (Baltimore: Johns Hopkins Press, 1991).

3 Gerard Manley Hopkins, Poem 69, *The Poems of Gerard Manley Hopkins*, 4th ed. (London: Oxford University Press, 1967). I am indebted to Carolyn Kizer for directing me to this poem by Hopkins and to Stevie Smith.

4 See, for example, George Boas, *The Cult of Childhood* (London: Warburg Institute, 1966). For a thoughtful perspective on the child metaphor as a whole, see James Hillman, "Abandoning the Child," in *Loose Ends: Primary Papers in Archetypal Psychology* (Zurich: Spring Publications, 1975).

CHAPTER 2

10 Richard Wilhelm and Cary F. Baynes, *I Ching* (Princeton, N.J.: Princeton University Press, 1971), p. 16.

12 William Stafford, *Writing the Australian Crawl*, quoted in *The Writer*, February 1982, p. 17.

12 Philip Roth, *The Ghost Writer* (New York: Farrar, Straus and Giroux, 1979), pp. 17–18.

17 Natalia Ginzburg, "Silence," in *The Little Virtues*, trans. Dick Davis (New York: Seaver Books, 1985), pp. 72–73.

21 Fritz Perls, *Gestalt Therapy Verbatim*, ed. John O. Stevens (New York: Bantam Books, 1972), p. 22.

CHAPTER 3

27 Samuel Taylor Coleridge, letter quoted in *Poetical Works of S. T. Coleridge*, ed. James Dykes Campbell (London: Macmillan and Co., 1938), p. iv.

29 Stanislaw Jerzy Lec, *Alle Unfrisierte Gedanken* [Uncombed Thoughts], ed. Karl Dedecius (Munich: Carl Hauser, 1982), p. 66.

CHAPTER 4

35 Fritz Perls, *Gestalt Therapy Verbatim*, ed. John O. Stevens (New York: Bantam Books, 1971), pp. 20–21.

38 *The Journal of Eugène Delacroix*, trans. Walter Pach (New York: Crown Publishers, 1948), p. 89.

39 Perls, *Gestalt Therapy*, p. 19.

43 Muriel Schiffman, *Gestalt Self Therapy* (Menlo Park, Calif.: Self Therapy Press, 1971), p. 63.

45 Donald Newlove, *Those Drinking Days: Myself and Other Writers* (New York: Horizon Press, 1981), pp. 100–102.

46 Cocteau, *Writers at Work*, p. 68.

47 Christopher Isherwood, interview, *Writers at Work: The Paris Review Interviews*, 4th series, ed. George Plimpton (New York: Penguin Books, 1976), p. 219.

47 Joyce Carol Oates, interview, *Women Writers at Work: The Paris Review Interviews*, ed. George Plimpton (Harmondsworth, England: Penguin, 1989), p. 366.

CHAPTER 5

48 Cyril Connolly, *Enemies of Promise* (New York: Macmillan, 1948), p. 87.

49 William Searle, editorial, *Occident*, Fall 1963, p. 4.

50 Robert Graves, interview, *Writers at Work: The Paris Review Interviews*,

4th series, ed. George Plimpton (New York: Penguin Books, 1976), p. 65.

52 Jorge Luis Borges, interview, *Writers at Work: The Paris Review Interviews*, 4th series, ed. George Plimpton (New York: Penguin Books, 1977), p. 123.

54 Evelyn Waugh, "Urbane Enjoyment Personified: Sir Osbert Sitwell," in *A Little Order*, ed. Donat Gallagher (Boston: Little, Brown, 1977), p. 97.

56 Cynthia Ozick, quoted in Helen Benedict, "A Writer's First Readers," *New York Times Book Review*, February 6, 1983, p. 11.

58 See *A Very Private Eye: Letters and Diaries of Barbara Pym*, ed. Hazel Holt and Hilary Pym (New York: E. P. Dutton, 1984), p. 213.

59 "Conversation with Diane Wakoski," *Hawaii Review*, Fall 1979, p. 27.

60 Philip Larkin, interview, *Writers at Work: The Paris Review Interviews*, 7th series, ed. George Plimpton (New York: Viking, 1986), p. 154.

60 Cynthia Ozick, interview, *Women Writers at Work: The Paris Review Interviews*, ed. George Plimpton (Harmondsworth, England: Penguin, 1989), p. 303.

61 Rainer Maria Rilke, *Letters*, vol. 1, trans. Jane Barnard Greene and M. D. Herter Norton (New York: W. W. Norton, 1947–48), p. 319.

61 I have been unable to verify this anecdote, but the comments of one scholar on the salubrious effect of Monet's obsessive late retouchings are instructive: "It was in the last stages of finishing his paintings that Monet was able to recreate the web of harmonies which he . . . felt connecting all parts of the natural scene" (John House, *Monet: Nature into Art*, New Haven: Yale University Press, 1986, p. 182).

CHAPTER 6

63 John Leggett, *Ross and Tom: Two American Tragedies* (New York: Simon and Schuster, 1974), p. 116.

64 Norman Mailer, *Advertisements for Myself* (New York: G. P. Putnam's Sons, 1959), p. 477; Harold Brodkey quoted in Edward Rothstein, "Look Homeward, Angel," *New York Review of Books*, February 15, 1990, p. 36.

65 Katherine Mansfield, *The Letters and Journals: A Selection*, ed. C. K. Stead (Hammondsworth, England: Penguin Books, 1977), p. 234.

66 Quoted in Aileen Ward, *John Keats: The Making of a Poet* (New York: Viking, 1963), p. 84.

66 Davy, about Coleridge, quoted in *Poetical Works of S. T. Coleridge*, ed. James Dykes Campbell (London: Macmillan & Co., 1938).

67 Ozick, *Women Writers at Work*, p. 300.

68 James Joyce, *A Portrait of the Artist as a Young Man* (New York: Viking Press, 1956), p. 253.

68 The phrase is Donald Newlove's. *Those Drinking Days: Myself and Other Writers* (New York: Horizon Press, 1981), p. 138.

69 Anaïs Nin, *Diaries: 1934–1939*, vol. 2, ed. Gunther Stuhlmann (New York: Harcourt, Brace and World, 1967), p. 20.

69 Lawrence Durrell, quoted in "Beating Writer's Block," *Time*, October 31, 1977, p. 101.

69 Lec, *Uncombed Thoughts*, p. 172.

70 Newlove, *Those Drinking Days*, pp. 125, 126.

70 Cyril Connolly, *Enemies of Promise* (New York: Macmillan, 1948), p. 106.

71 Newlove, *Those Drinking Days*, p. 125.

71 Tom Dardis, *The Thirsty Muse: Alcohol and the American Writer* (New York: Ticknor & Fields, 1989).

72 Delmore Schwartz, quoted in James Atlas, *Delmore Schwartz: The Life of an American Poet* (New York: Avon Books, 1978), p. 175.

72 Charles Jackson, *The Lost Weekend* (New York: Noonday Press, 1960), p. 46.

73 Newlove, *Those Drinking Days*, p. 125.

73 Charles Lamb, "Sanity of True Genius," *Complete Works and Letters* (New York: Random House, 1935), p. 167.

75 Ward, *John Keats*, p. 260–61.

75 See the discussion of Wordsworth's inflation in, for example, M. H. Abrams, *Natural Supernaturalism* (New York: W. W. Norton, 1971).

CHAPTER 7

76 Frances Cornford, "Youth," *Collected Poems* (London: Cresset Press, 1954), p. 14.

76 Wendell Berry, "Poetry and Marriage," in *Standing by Words* (San Francisco: North Point Press, 1983), p. 204.

78 Milan Kundera, *The Book of Laughter and Forgetting* (New York: Penguin Books, 1981), p. 106.

78 Marie Louise von Franz, *Puer Aeternus* (New York: Spring Publications, 1970), p. 2. My discussion of the *puer aeternus* figure is indebted to von Franz's ground-breaking analysis.

80 Robert Musil, *The Man Without Qualities* (London: Pan, 1979), vol. 1, p. 297; vol. 2, p. 33.

80 This discussion draws from Daphne du Maurier's *The Infernal World of Branwell Brontë* (New York: Pocket Books, 1962).

81 Quoted in John Livingston Lowes, *The Road to Xanadu*, 2nd rev. ed. (London: Constable, 1951), p. 21.

CHAPTER 8

86 George Eliot, *Middlemarch* (New York: Harcourt, Brace and World, 1962), p. 273.

86 See Carobeth Laird, *Encounter with an Angry God* (New York: Ballantine Books, 1977).

88 Natalia Ginzburg, "My Vocation," in *The Little Virtues,* trans. Dick Davis (New York: Seaver Books, 1986), p. 66.

89 Rollo May, *The Courage to Create* (New York: W. W. Norton, 1975), pp. 69–70. The italics are mine.

90 Frank O'Connor, interview, *Writers at Work: The Paris Review Interviews,* 1st series, ed. Malcolm Cowley (New York: Penguin Books, 1958), p. 168.

90 Anthony Burgess, interview, *Writers at Work: The Paris Review Interviews,* 4th series, ed. George Plimpton (New York: Penguin Books, 1977), p. 332.

92 Fyodor Dostoevsky, letter to A. V. Korvin-Krukovskaya, excerpted in *Crime and Punishment,* trans. Jessie Coulson (rev.), ed. George Gibian (New York: W. W. Norton, 1975), p. 480ff.

92 Burgess, *Writers at Work,* p. 344.

94 John Steinbeck, *Journal of a Novel: The East of Eden Letters* (New York: Viking, 1969), p. 84.

94 Eileen Simpson, *Poets in Their Youth: A Memoir* (New York: Random House, 1982), p. 93.

95 Anne Tyler, quoted in Helen Benedict, "A Writer's First Readers," *New York Times Book Review,* February 6, 1983, p. 24.

CHAPTER 9

98 Gérard de Nerval, letter to George Bell, quoted in Richard Holmes, *Footsteps: Adventures of a Romantic Biographer* (London: Hodder and Stoughton, 1985).

98 William T. Vollman, "The Grave of Lost Stories," in Patrick McGrath and Bradford Morrow, eds., *The New Gothic* (New York: Random House, 1991), p. 316.

99 Norman Mailer, *Cannibals and Christians* (New York: Dial Press, 1966), p. 124.

101 Cyril Connolly, *Enemies of Promise* (New York: Macmillan, 1948), p. 24.

105 Gore Vidal, "French Letters: Theories of the New Novel," in *Homage to Daniel Shays: Collected Essays 1952–1972* (New York: Vintage Books, 1973), p. 279.

106 S. J. Perelman, interview, *Writers at Work: The Paris Review Interviews,* 2nd series, ed. George Plimpton (New York: Penguin Books, 1982), p. 248.

CHAPTER 10

107 Edward Albee, interview, *Writers at Work: The Paris Review Interviews,* 3rd series, ed. George Plimpton (New York: Penguin Books, 1977), p. 328.

110 Jorge Luis Borges, interview, *Writers at Work: The Paris Review Inter-*

views, 4th series, ed. George Plimpton (New York: Penguin Books, 1976), p. 123.

113 Rilke, *Letters*, vol. 1, p. 318.

114 Tom Wolfe, *The Kandy-Colored Tangerine-Flake Streamline Baby* (New York: Farrar, Straus and Giroux, 1965), ix–xii.

115 May Sarton, interview, *Writers at Work: The Paris Review Interviews*, 7th series, ed. George Plimpton (New York: Viking, 1986).

116 *The Notebooks of Joseph Joubert: A Selection*, ed. and trans. Paul Auster (San Francisco: North Point Press, 1983). I was first directed to Joubert by Thomas Farber. See his *Compared to What? On Writing and the Writer's Life* (New York: W. W. Norton, 1988), p. 75.

CHAPTER 11

118 Virginia Woolf, *Three Guineas* (New York: Harcourt, Brace and Co., 1938), p. 217. I was directed to this quote from Tillie Olsen's *Silences*.

120 James Baldwin, in *Conversations with James Baldwin*, ed. Fred L. Standley and Louis H. Pratt (Jackson and London: University of Mississippi Press, 1989), p. 208.

120 Toni Morrison, *Playing in the Dark: Whiteness and the Literary Imagination* (Cambridge: Harvard University Press, 1992), x–xi.

121 Milton Murayama, quoted in Franklin S. Odo, afterword to *All I Asking for Is My Body* (Honolulu: University of Hawaii Press, 1988), p. 105.

125 Evelyn White, quoted in Carolyn Harris, "Breaking Silence: The Women's Writing Series," *Radcliffe News*, Summer 1992, p. 11.

127 Tillie Olsen, *Silences* (New York: Delacorte Press/Seymour Lawrence, 1978), p. 38.

CHAPTER 12

129 Tadeusz Konwicki, *A Minor Apocalypse*, trans. Richard Lourie (New York: Farrar, Straus and Giroux, 1983), p. 3.

130 S. I. Witkiewicz *père* quoted in Daniel Gerould, *Witkacy: Stanislaw Ignacy Witkiewicz as an Imaginative Writer* (Seattle and London: University of Washington Press, 1981), p. 24.

132 Milan Kundera, *Life Is Elsewhere*, trans. Peter Kussi (New York: Alfred A. Knopf, 1974), p. 205.

133 John Stuart Mill, *Autobiography* (New York: Columbia University Press, 1960), pp. 97, 93.

133 Stephen Shrader, *Leaving by the Closet Door* (Iowa City: University of Iowa Press, 1968).

137 Natalia Ginzburg, "My Vocation," in *The Little Virtues*, p. 66.

137 *The Diaries of Franz Kafka 1910–1913*, ed. Max Brod (New York: Schocken Books, 1965), p. 33.

139 Louise Bogan, *Journey Around My Room: The Autobiography of Louise Bogan*, ed. Ruth Limmer, (New York: Viking, 1980), p. 116.

140 Robert Lowell, "Hopkins's Sanctity," in *Collected Prose* (New York: Farrar Straus and Giroux, 1986), p. 168.

140 Heinrich von Kleist, in Joachim Maass, *Kleist: A Biography*, trans. Ralph Manheim (New York: Farrar, Straus and Giroux, 1983), p. 47.

141 Lec, *Uncombed Thoughts*, frontispiece quote.

141 Douglas Day, *Malcolm Lowry: A Biography* (New York: Oxford University Press, 1973), p. 72.

143 Cyril Connolly, *Enemies of Promise* (New York: Macmillan, 1948), p. 111.

143 Rainer Maria Rilke, *Letters*, vol. 1, trans. Jane Barnard Greene and M. D. Herter Norton (New York: W. W. Norton, 1947–48), p. 300.

CHAPTER 13

144 Gina Berriault, *The Lights of Earth* (San Francisco: North Point Press, 1984), pp. 22–23.

145 Saul Bellow, interview, *Writers at Work: The Paris Review Interviews*, 3rd series, ed. George Plimpton (New York: Penguin Books, 1975), p. 186.

150 Honore de Balzac, *Lost Illusions*, trans. Kathleen Raine (London: John Lehmann, 1951), pp. 258–260.

151 Stephen Spender, "Fame and the Poet," *New York Review of Books*, December 18, 1986, p. 75.

152 Cyril Connolly, quoted in "Beating Writer's Block," *Time*, October 31, 1977, p. 101.

152 Leo Braudy, *The Frenzy of Renown: Fame and Its History* (New York: Oxford University Press, 1986), p. 555.

153 James Baldwin, interview with Julius Lester, in *Conversations with James Baldwin*, p. 229.

154 Braudy, *Frenzy of Renown*, p. 539.

155 Cyril Connolly, *Enemies of Promise* (New York: Macmillan, 1948), p. 7.

155 See Ralph Maud, ed., introduction to *The Notebooks of Dylan Thomas* (New York: New Directions, 1967), p. 10.

155 John Raeburn, *Fame Became of Him: Hemingway as Public Writer* (Bloomington: Indiana University Press, 1984).

156 John Steinbeck, *Journal of a Novel: The East of Eden Letters* (New York: Viking, 1969), p. 6.

158 Randall Jarrell, introduction to *The Man Who Loved Children* by Christina Stead (New York: Holt, Rinehart and Winston, 1965), xxxix.

160 Jean Rhys, quoted in David Plante, *Difficult Women: A Memoir of Three* (New York: Atheneum, 1983), p. 22.

CHAPTER 14

162 Isak Dinesen, "The Blank Page," in *Last Tales* (New York: Random House, 1957), p. 100. Read the entire story to discover the scandalous significance of the "blank page."

163 Jean Cocteau, interview, *Writers at Work: The Paris Review Interviews,* 3rd series, ed. George Plimpton (New York: Penguin Books, 1975), pp. 66–69.

163 John Keats, *Letters,* ed. Robert Gittings (London: Oxford University Press, 1970), p. 65.

164 Rollo May, *The Courage to Create* (New York: W. W. Norton, 1975), p. 81.

165 Natalia Ginzburg, "My Vocation," in *The Little Virtues,* p. 66.

166 Leo Bersani, "A Tomb for Anatole," *New York Times Book Review,* January 15, 1984.

166 David Malouf, *Child's Play* (Ringwood, Victoria: Penguin Australia, 1983), p. 60.

167 Philip Larkin, *Writers at Work,* p. 174.

167 E. M. Forster, "Trooper Silas Tomkyn Comberbacke," *Abinger Harvest* (New York: Meridian Books, 1955), p. 216.

167 Elizabeth Bowen, *Collected Impressions* (New York: Alfred A. Knopf, 1950), p. 126.

169 Otto Rank, *The Myth of the Birth of the Hero* (New York: Vintage Books, 1959), p. 131.

APPENDIX

171 Samuel Taylor Coleridge, *Poems,* ed. Ernest Hartley Coleridge (London: Oxford University Press, 1960).

171 (note) See *The Nabokov–Wilson Letters,* ed. Simon Karlinsky (New York: Harper & Row, 1979), pp. 123, 169ff.

172 Robert Graves, *Collected Poems* (Garden City, N.Y.: Doubleday, 1961), p. 342.

172 Stevie Smith, *Selected Poems,* ed. James MacGibbon (London: Penguin Books, 1978), pp. 230–232.

Index

--- ❖ ---